Shambolic Tapestry

or

A history of a Somerset landscape
according to Mark Walker

Published by Honeybee Books
www.honeybeebooks.co.uk

Printed in the UK using paper from sustainable sources

ISBN: 978-1-913675-14-1

Preface

This book is based on the symbiotic relationship between humanity and all living plants and trees, from LUCA – the last universal common ancestor, from which all life evolved – to the present day. Fondly portrayed through three tree characters, Quercus (Oak), Fraxinus (Ash) and Corylus (Hazel), the book shows how they, like humans, have life struggles, differences and a story to tell. Little do we know or understand of our universe and what it's all about, so it's quite fitting that the story of the changing landscape is observed by the hidden eyes of three trees growing in southwest England.

The story reflects my personal thoughts and opinions. It's not meant to be a scholarly work or a source of detailed historical information.

I would like to dedicate this book to my good friend Richard, who gave me the space to breathe, and to thank Jody Lidgard, who gave me the title and inspiration for this story. I am also hugely indebted to Liz Hammond, who applied the polish to the book that made it shine, and provided the back cover synopsis. All of course in the randomly shambolic tapestry of life.

Contents

Introduction

My name is Mark Walker and I am a gardener from a small village in Somerset. I have been blessed with working in many gardens and treated them as my own. My philosophy of life is that we all end up the same and that we never truly own anything but just have the pleasure of being a guardian of our chosen home. Respect and love what we have around us and it will reward us in good time. So as I stand here on my beloved hillside overlooking my childhood village, I notice familiar landmarks, trees and plants all around me. Such memories make me smile and shed a tear, for they are emotions that in life you should truly embrace to fully call yourself a human being.

The most prominent and noticeable objects on the hillside are the trees. They are much older than me and have witnessed more goings on than I can ever dream about. They are the ancients and they have gained my true respect. So as my mindful moment of peace and relaxation fades, and my brain begins to think quite hard, I pause in a brief moment of time.

Hmm, I wonder, what if all the trees and plants on this childhood play area of mine had thoughts and feelings just like us? What would their story of life and evolution be, and is it any different from ours?

I wonder …   *(enters into a dreamy world)*

PART 1
EARLY BEGINNINGS

In the beginning

'Let there be light' were some of the first words in the Bible. They could on the other hand symbolise the Big Bang from which our universe was formed. We as humans are still exploring and soul-searching both entities for answers to what it's all about, the meaning of life, who we are and what our purpose is. The concept of LUCA (last universal common ancestor – the most recent group of organisms from which all existing life descended) was born from scientific understanding of all of creation, from the study of all known organisms.

We humans are as much a part of nature as the trees, plants and animals on our unique and special planet. Our fortunate beginning was mastered by the stars themselves, and to understand it fully is to be truly complete in our personal quest for knowledge. The plants, insects and indeed the animals are less forthcoming in sharing their ideals and secrets with us fully. Only time will tell if we eventually get it.

Our existence, as far as we know, makes us the only highly intelligent species within our universe – well, until someone else turns up in the meantime. They could have already been here but decided to be antisocial and failed to knock on the door for a cup of tea. If that's the case then let them be ignorant, as we are not much better, and indeed we're probably less hospitable given humankind's track record of peace. Now if a race of ETs had decided to greet us they would probably have taken plant samples plus the odd cow in order to research our kind, knowing that our genetics or seed are all from the same origin.

What we do know is that our planet, along with our sun, is billions of years old, and probably a lot more if we had all the facts in front of us. We can just guess at this point, but anyway what's a few billion years between friends? Now I'm not going to go into the science of how we acquired an atmosphere, rain, and fluffy clouds, as this would take me far too long to finally finish this book (I say this after just page one). Bear with me though – it gets better!

Jurassic period

As a proper down to earth gardener and horticulturist I can only see the planet from my humble beginnings. I like to think that nature along with our rugged landscape holds the answers to all the planet's history, from the bare open spaces on the highlands to the rocky footpaths within a shaded woodland. From day dot they haven't changed much, give and take the odd volcanic eruption and earthquake plus intercontinental plate shifts. Ok, ok, it's probably not the same, but that's all I can see in front of me at this present time. Earth first achieved a habitable atmosphere in which we all began to evolve. Chuck in a good measure of water and sunlight and you have the recipe for bacteria and fungi and salt to form something that resembles life. The earth was a big combination of rocks forged from the furnaces of the universe itself, and this gave us all a firm footing on which to build the first signs of life. From the seas came the lizards who had managed to turn their fins into feet and stunted hands – they were to become known to us as dinosaurs. They ruled over the planet for billions of years, some meat eaters, others vegetarians. Each one had a purpose and was part of the natural food chain. They seemed intelligent within their own world of kill or be killed. We like to think that the T-Rex was the dominant force of their time but it could have easily been the insects or indeed the plants?

You see, from the start plants, trees and insects have always been there. They all had the first house party, the grand opening ceremony. They invented pollination and breathed out oxygen for all those with a lung to enjoy, and indeed we and animals breathed out carbon dioxide for the plants to soak up and enjoy. The sun just helped these solar harvesters to gorge on their own food production; within that, folks, is photosynthesis, but enough of the science, let's stick to the programme, shall we? Anyway you get where I'm coming from: we need plants, they need us. To spoil that would mean the end to all we have begun and that's been gifted to us from the wonderful universe.

The dinosaurs had no great big plan other than pure survival from day to day. Their pea-size brain and reptile mentality meant their purpose on the planet had to be disrupted by something really big to knock them off their pedestal. Front and centre stage bring a massive asteroid hurtling towards the Earth, probably on the rebound from the Big Bang itself. Like all things in life what goes around comes around. I'm not saying those huge reptiles deserved it. Being that our planet is as fragile as a soap bubble within a field of fluffy cotton means that we are all defenceless to what the universe can decide to throw back at us from time to time. Admittedly our atmosphere burns up most of the comets unlucky enough to be grabbed by our gravity, while the moon without its atmosphere just takes it like a punch-drunk boxer, leaving its surface looking like a bad dose of acne. But hey, when you get these big asteroids coming along you just got to batten down the hatches and roll with the punches. This scenario was just bad luck for the unsuspecting dinosaurs. To think one day they were chewing on a bone or a big monkey puzzle, then bang, blackout. You see given the massive dent within the Caribbean ocean, this asteroid was big – big enough to create huge tidal waves and a dust cloud that was strong enough to block out the sun's light for hundreds of years. Along with the subsequent earthquakes and volcanoes the dinosaurs really didn't stand a chance. This lack of light destabilised the fragile equilibrium of life for plants, the plant eaters plus the eaters that ate the vegetarians, not to mention triggering an ice age that would plunge the planet into a deep freeze. As the dinosaurs were initially cold-blooded but developed through evolution into warm-blooded, they were once again a victim of their own success given the big freeze.

From this cataclysmic series of events most of life on Earth was either made extinct or forced to adapt to its surroundings. The birds were first to adapt; their ability to cover great expanses very quickly and migrate to the ideal feeding ground gave them the greatest chance of survival. The trees and plants on the other hand died where they stood, leaving only the really fortunate ones within the best location a chance to carry on as normal. This big freeze, though, just put everything into stasis until the planet had repaired itself. The seeds within the ground from the last harvest would eventually live to fight another day – they all just had to bide their time. Such Jurassics would be the ferns of this world along with ginkgoes and conifers, which held firm to pass down their knowledge to the next genera-tion of plants yet to be born. They started singing songs to themselves like 'We are the champions', 'Another one bites the dust' and one about a dance called the fandango? You're right, plants are weird.

The ice age
The big freeze sorted the men from the mice with most of the northern and southern hemisphere locked in a blanket of snow and ice. This cooled

the planet down and slowed down any future species evolution, which gave the planet a kind of a reset where no one really claimed dominance over the planet's future. The plants would hold out in the ground under the ice but the equatorial areas like parts of Africa would have a slight advantage over most plant life. The mammals and birds were present, but confined to just the best areas, suitable for their evolution. The planet had also taken on a major shift in its appearance, in the shape of new continents. These were created by the continental plates of the planet continually shifting upwards or outwards. Land mass was slowly wrenched apart to create individual continents. The thaw would gradually start to reveal the full picture of the planet's new look, which also started to introduce the forms of species and life eagerly awaiting their turn to shine on the planet.

Humankind was one such species that was keen to make an impression on the planet's future. Now I'm not wishing to upset any religious people or scientific professors on how we came to being on this planet; I will leave that up to you the reader to decide what's right or wrong, just buy the book please! Monkeys and man, trees and plants – all the same in my eyes. We all share the same place on this planet and breathe the same air. All I know is that humankind's evolution, like the giant reptiles before, was born from the sea. Land gave us all a firm footing to grow on and the plants gave us substance to eat. Without any of this we would still be swimming in the water waiting for the next catch to come along.

Given that the Earth is spherical, the Equator had the most heat from the sun's rays. Further north or south away from the Equator, the land warmed much more gradually, and this gave us temperate zones as we know them today. Africa was deemed to be the breadbasket of the world, where humankind started their journey of discovery. The earliest skulls of humans were found in places like Somalia, so let's start from there.

Human race

As humankind evolved they started to straighten up their backs and be prepared for all the hard work in front of them. They were keen to get on and make their presence known. They possessed something that all mammals and animals and indeed plants lacked – this was a brain that continued to get better the more they learnt, primarily as a tool to hunt and kill both their prey plus anyone they really didn't like. Humans were a competitive species that just wanted to be top dog within their harem of females and amongst their tribe. This primeval instinct had got them out of the trees and onto the plains. I'm not sure if humans started off as meat eaters or veggies; all I know is without the two we can't grow strong and healthy. Plants on the other hand set out the table for the humans long before the humans had arrived. This preparation meant that humans had something to eat when they got hungry before their need for meat overpowered them. Plants were around when the dinosaurs ruled, and they just wanted to carry on the service for humans. The trouble is the humans, like the dinosaurs, took it all for granted – they never realised that this is a partnership that would be locked in a fixed contract for all time, well at least until that asteroid turns up again. Humankind was as strong as an ox being that they were all brand new, and their instincts of smell, hearing and sight gave them great advantage when weeding out the weaker species. Strong arms and powerful legs gave them flexibility to cover most land areas quickly, and they had yet to need the comforts of clothes or shelter as they were still a hairy race with a thick skin. The sun gave them warmth, the sky provided them with water, and a tree gave them shelter when both got a little too much.

Trees and plants on the other hand, or shall I say branch or stem, were slow movers. Their seed genetics meant they had to grow where they stood within the soil provided by a previous plant's death or the annual shed of leaf or stem. They like humans required the warmth of the sun plus the rain from the sky to survive, but for them it was all so different. We as humans evolved one massive organ of skin to cover our calcium-filled bone frame which encases our organs like heart, kidneys, etc. Our brains compute and organise all of these parts to work to the best of our ability given the situation. Nerves give us the feeling of touch and smell, and our brains then tell us to keep warm or put on deodorant. Plants as far as I know do not possess any visible organs; they are one big organ of growth, well at least until I'm told differently. The thing is their secrets are kept close to the stems. Humans are very self-explanatory, well for some of us anyway.

From the moment a plant germinates from its seed its sole purpose is to head downwards or inwards to something it can grow from. Plants' initial tap root makes the first move, followed by a number of spurs or lateral roots. This creates an anchor in the ground to begin the feast of the ground's nutrients and moisture. Once they have established a firm footing they create stems upwards. They then choose to head further upwards, crossways or trailing depending on their given genetics. They then produce their solar harvesters to do something really magical for me. This is when they start to think about producing a flower and food. Through a mixture of water and carbon dioxide they produce a pigment known as chlorophyll from which their fine machine produces oxygen. This process, called photosynthesis, produces sugars which are stored in their natural larder, only to be released or raided when the plant needs them to produce more leaf and stem. Now our understanding of plants has made us realise that we need the plants to produce oxygen in the air but they need us all to breathe out carbon dioxide. This never-ending circle of production helps us all to maintain a healthy clean atmosphere within our planet.

Going back to when I said that plants have no visible organs, well the Amazon rainforest and all jungles of the planet are represented as the lungs of the planet. Their collection of trees and plants also transpire excess water through the pores in their leaf surface on which they create humidity and moisture within the air. Plants big or small also contribute to the balance of other plants through pollination, aided by the unsung heroes called insects – they need these little workers to pollinate their flowers. Once this has been achieved the plant can rest until the following year when the process starts all over again. Their unique manufacturing, all from a tiny seed, is truly brilliant, and their life span can be long or short depending on what they are genetically gifted. Things like the towering trees can easily outgrow a human, but with such a slow growth rate, they are in no hurry to get anywhere in particular. A fortnight on the other hand can be a very important time for a plant: as it sets out its stall in floral brilliance to attract the local bees, it puts faith in nature to help it see a following year. Three months of growing can all be lost if the insects are not passing by, shopping for pollen to produce their food source of honey. Thankfully the planet in its infancy had an abundance of all until humankind had other plans.

Plants divided themselves into groups like annual, perennial and evergreens so that they could ensure insects, humans and animals always had something to eat or chew on whatever the season. Humankind feasted on the fruits of the plants' labour, giving themselves valuable energy from the plants' sugary attributes like berries and the protein of nuts. This made humans grow strong and tall along with the odd bit of wind and stomach ache if they gorged too much.

Not all plants were edible though, and this is where some curious human met his match and paid the highest cost just to satisfy his greedy curiosity. I suppose someone had to experiment so that humans could learn not to eat that particular plant. These plants did this so that they could avoid being wiped out by anyone or anything wishing to nibble on their colourful berry or leaf. Self-preservation comes in all shapes and forms.

The thaw

The big thaw of the planet began very slowly. Our orbit around the sun meant that we all experienced mini glacial periods divided into the four seasons of winter, spring, summer and autumn within a full year. Humans and plants adapted to all four seasons really well and expected it as the norm. The jungles of the equatorial ranges never fully experienced this, noticing only a slight change in probably a bit more rain than usual, but as the jungles are always damp and humid no one really complained. It was the northern and southern hemisphere regions that started to benefit from the temperature change. A day of awakening was starting to unfurl within the frozen ice beds of northern Europe, revealing totally fresh and different landscapes. The compact ice and snow had over millions of years gouged out great valleys and gorges, the once ice sheets of Europe revealing their bare rocky skeleton forged by the planet's movement over millennia. Frozen in stasis were the seeds and plants from yesteryear which the spring warmth would crack open from their hibernation.

Life had been reinstated along with a dictionary full of plant varieties that to us in modern times are seen all over our countryside. The air was crisp and clean with a gentle warmth of sun forcing the tiny seeds to reset time. Try to imagine them all yawning in a symbiotic tune to one another, all greeting and meeting familiar plants with the first open stem into leaf then flower. This very small moment for the plants was truly a big deal to them as they were the reborn pioneers of the land when no available substrate of topsoil was present. Their first struggle was to seek out nutrients and moisture left over from the last season's growth within a layer of rock. Some would naturally fail, others would seek a hairline crack to puncture the rock's surface. They felt sorry for their fallen cousins but it was safety in numbers – if they succeeded millions would flourish after them and their story would begin again. They noticed that their environment was a lot different to their ancestors', with no big reptiles and no sound other than the odd fleeting bird in the sky. They could relate to the birds but everything seemed so miniature (which seems strange, I know, coming from a small seed) but evolution had dealt these seeds an open field of hope. They all relished their new setting, they were so pleased to have a second chance of life from the generous universe. They remembered fondly their first incarnation like it was yesterday; for some reason though this seemed much better than the first time as they had a wealth of genetic code to utilise within this new world.

So as they all collectively stood tall within their miniature world, a connection was made through their roots, like when we humans hold hands and tickle bare feet together. Happily they all giggled amongst themselves like little munchkins, then sighed a sigh of relief. They seemed to communicate through the pulses of the soil in a way totally alien to us humans. Not all of them got the same start in life, some having to really dig deep to find any form of comfort within the earth, others thinking that was easy compared with the big boulders they had to bypass before they could stretch out their roots. Some of them hadn't even got out of bed yet. Sounds familiar?

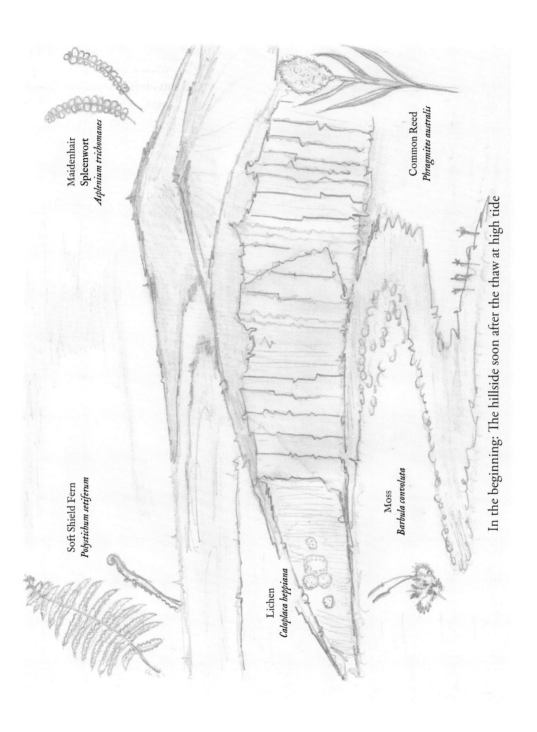

Maidenhair
Spleenwort
Asplenium trichomanes

Common Reed
Phragmites australis

Soft Shield Fern
Polystichum setiferum

Lichen
Caloplaca heppiana

Moss
Barbula convoluta

In the beginning: The hillside soon after the thaw at high tide

PART 2
INTRODUCING THE HILLTOP

The hilltop

So the scene is set on an open hilltop within the south-west region of what we know as England. It's a standard hilltop no different to any other hilltop within the country or indeed the whole planet, but this is my hilltop, a place which would eventually inspire me to write this story; well we have to start somewhere anyway. It was a place where the freshness of the air met the clean crisp cool ground, all brand new and hopeful for the future's inhabitants. I base this feeling on sowing seeds in a tray of freshly made loam or compost; pat it down dry, smell the earth and wait for the new arrivals to appear. The plants all initiated their production mechanism – they worked very quickly to achieve phase one of germination. The spring season gave this initial kickstart and growth was steadily improving as the weeks went by.

First to set out the table were the fescues and bents or grasses of the hill. They for some reason had first dibs on the virgin ground; it seemed just right for this to happen. They both grew very quickly on a hilltop despite lacking all the correct nutrient levels to survive. Within a month they had stretched upwards to the sky with an equal amount of root within the ground; some though grew stunted with a faded colour due to a stubborn hardened rock beneath. This didn't faze them as the overall look from space gave the hilltop a hue of green, and they were just keen to impress their creators with a dogged determination. Their presence the world over would begin to change the landscape dramatically – some large, some small, all green and translucent. Grasses the planet over had a unique gene that gave them toughness in extreme conditions along with a need to withstand most abuse thrown at them. As they reached maximum height on the solar equinox of summer they began to unfurl their hidden insignificant flower heads with equally hidden stamens and seed engine.

This safety in numbers idea worked well as their annual seed sow meant that their first year was a total success, covering a larger area as the seasons progressed. As they had their fill of the planet's atmosphere plus the ground's nutrients they would all sway gently in the wind showing off a wave of red and pink shades. This was the canvas beginning of what would be the shambolic tapestry of the ancient hillside – others soon would join in with this merry dance of colour. Hidden towards the lower margins of the hill, where the soil was much moister, was a collection of wild orchids, then on a slow downward slope to the stream's edge lay the willow herbs and nettles. Their flow would complete the symphony of colour that benefits all the insects and wildlife to a T. Their inner machine of sugars gave them a matured appearance before their retirement downwards into the ground. Once their job had been done the autumn and winter's wrath would slowly degrade their once strong, hollow stems, causing them to collapse on the ground in pure exhaustion. The winter frosts and cold nights would then trigger their hibernation in the ground leaving their empty husk above ground to form a layer of the hillside's first compost.

Slowly but gradually, after many, many seasons had passed, a generous layer of fine topsoil had been created, all helped along by the tunnelling worms and ants who would seek refuge within the spoils of the grasses' success. The fescues and bents would welcome these insects willingly as they provided their roots with valuable microbes, plus aerated the soil. And it was the grasses' friendly, unsuspecting neighbours that would introduce new plants within their sea of green pasture: the ants liked the taste of some seeds, which made them cover large areas of ground to find them. These highly strong, underestimated little insects would work like Trojans to bring back a fallen seed pod four times their size, on their backs or in their jaws over great distances, then store them underground in large larder stores for future feasts. The ant hills that were formed by the excavation of their subterranean homes were, depending on their species, a work of fine art or a bulldozed mass of spoil. They provided a unique loamy soil in which a collection of seeds would naturally germinate, restarting the cycle of life within its core.

The birds and the bees

The planet has always had a food chain, with us currently right at the top. We as humankind took this all for granted from our early existence; I suppose though if it's already been there for us, we do what is natural and eat it. Plants gave a substance to keep us on the right track both physically

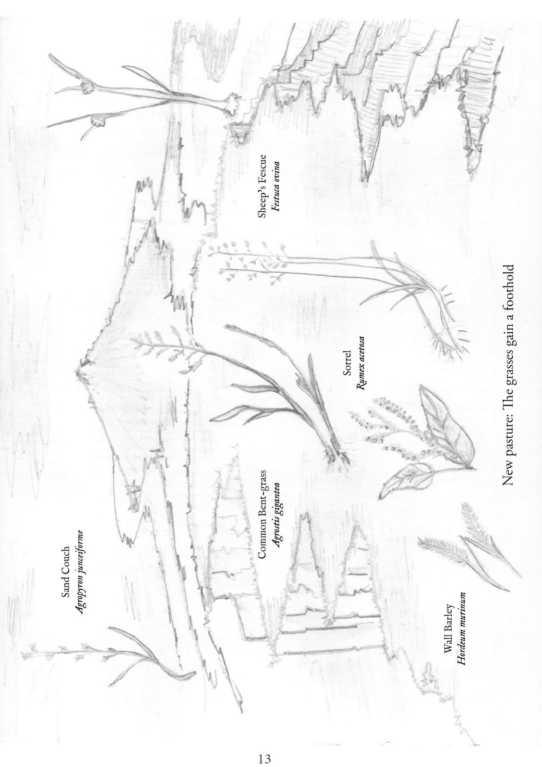

Sheep's Fescue
Festuca ovina

Sorrel
Rumex acetosa

Sand Couch
Agropyron junceiforme

Common Bent-grass
Agrostis gigantea

Wall Barley
Hordeum murinum

New pasture: The grasses gain a foothold

13

and mentally, and meat came later as we experimented with flint and rock for weapons. Plants just provided us with a launch pad to grow from. Now the insects of the world have, as far as I can look back in time, always been present in some shape or form. Even the humble bumblebee has evolved from its Jurassic roots, initially being a carnivore, then turning into a pollen-eating herbivore. All these changes so that we can have honey on our toast. Insects helped the plants get on with their business in the world, but for me they are the smallest cog that holds everything together. They are the underdogs of the world, the true workforce that makes the planet tick, and without them we simply wouldn't be here. Their shift patterns are relentless just as long as there are plants to work on, be it through pollination or laying their own eggs for future colonies. Deemed as a pest with the stigma of bringing an unclean environment into our clean modern homes, they just continue to piss us off with their merry dance around the lampshade. Not quite sure if they ever get dizzy? The reality, though, is that they were here first and we must just get on with them. Plants truly need insects to survive and we need plants for us to survive.

The ants are an organised battalion of greatness within the insect world, small in stature but they had high hopes. Just sometimes though the British weather would spoil their little homes in the form of heavy rain on the hillside – this sudden deluge of moisture would flood their subterranean community, forcing them to flee their homes in a sudden mad panic. Ants were totally used to this after many years of this happening to them within their lifetime, so they just took it on the chin and moved home just as soon as the weather changed. They were pragmatic realists in the face of adversity: let's start a new tunnel elsewhere – the weather would never suspect it (visions of *The Great Escape*). Left in the ground in the aftermath, buried within the blended topsoil, would be the fruit of their labour from a distant field carried by a chain of ant colonies the country over. This seed transfer from each colony would then eventually find home on our hillside full of grasses amongst the worms and the singing birds. Probably too perfect so early on within the book; I really can't help myself, you know.

The birds of this world are the remnants of the Jurassic period, like most animals, and mammals alike evolved into who they are over millions of years. Albeit a lot smaller than their ancestors, birds had the gift of flight which enabled them to migrate to areas suitable for their breeding and nesting needs. They split up and created many varieties in groups like finch, gull and sparrow, some with a dominant territorial nature towards their cousins. Some types of birds were flightless, but all laid eggs like the reptiles before them, this external womb making them vulnerable to loss from other predators and indeed birds of their kind. Their nests consisted of twigs and moss all cleverly built by a weaving beak, strong enough to withstand wind and rain high up in a tree or within the thorny spikes of a hedge. The job for male and female was to keep their eggs warm until incubation of their young was just right for them to break free. They nonetheless were survivors that provided us with the first dawn chorus plus a rude awakening call when we decide to lie in from time to time. Musicians would try to mimic their songs but seldom replicated them. This was *their* birdsong that could not be downloaded; their communication with their breed held a unique code only understandable by themselves. It's funny to watch them outside on our lawn patrolling their patch, with one eye on the worm, the other watching me watching them. Well back in time to the hillside. The blackbird was one such tenacious species of bird that would be totally alert at all times, both to a predator and to worms rising whilst it searched a wet field.

This would be the start of an invasion from land and sky; the grasses really couldn't have it all their way on a hillside open to attack. As the grasses laid down the building blocks of growth, they were about to become victims of their own success, and this came in two ways. First, the travelling birds would drop their payload of waste from the sky. Within their waste lay some undigested seed pod from a short distance away in the form of sorrel seeds. This British native had no idea it would be airdropped behind enemy lines in such an unceremonious fashion. But nature had dealt the sorrel a unique chance to spread her seed away from the confines of home in the counties further south. Underground, on the other hand, lurked another dormant plant known to us affectionately as buttercup. Her kidnapping from the borders of the lower Levels on the back of a migrant colony of ants would be a surreal awakening. She adapted well to the slight climate change and was only too keen to begin the work of punching her way out of the grasses' stranglehold. Buttercup would have the added advantage of creeping amongst the grasses, weaving her stems to an open space not occupied by the fescue to restart a new flower stem. Her secret weapon would be to hunt out potassium deposits plus slowly impair other plant life around her – charming but deceitful, plus adaptable like the grasses to most environmental stresses. The grasses welcomed their uninvited cousin as they knew that they had to try and out-compete her if they were to truly rule the hillside. Let battle commence.

Sorrel had the element of surprise as she was airdropped in by the black-bird. This payload consisted of the bird's waste that held the seed within, and when this weapon was deployed, sorrel would be flying in blind to her new location. Touchdown was perfect, between two swords of grass. Sorrel had luck on her side, as others before her were left spread out over the tops of the grass stems. Others would be blown off course onto a lone rock without any means to anchor for germination into any soil – well, on the big scale of things there is a lot of hit and miss the world over, given the amount of birds in the sky.

For sorrel Lady Luck was shining on her, along with another new addition of plantain, her journey similar but with the help of a rook. Their random dispersal within a few metres of each other was the beginning of a shambolic tapestry of plants that without the hand of humankind created their own portrait of how plants do things around here. Within a few seasons of give and take between the three plants, a blanket of colour from early spring right up to late autumn was clearly visible. The insects joined in quite happily above and below ground as their eggs and colonies continued to grow. It's hard though for me to truly understand or feel the goings on in the field as I walk through in present time – I just enjoy what's in front of me. Through its perfect setting it's hard to believe any arguments or fighting between the plants is happening, purely as I gauge this against the madness of a big city or jammed motorway. Let's just see, shall we?

So as the quiet invasion started and buttercup and fescue began to lock horns, a heated argument arose. Fescue was a proud species of plant that had had her own way for many years, and she would make comments like 'Bloody foreigners, turning up unannounced then taking over MY field without a moment's notice. Who do they think they are?' Buttercup on the other hand was a victim of natural migration and was unexpectedly forced to take root in a land most alien to herself. She had to just get on with what life had dealt her and try to make the best out of a bad situation. At first the two plants tried to avoid each other but a confrontation was on the cards with the odds stacked in fescue's favour. This is what happened one wet and cloudy day within the meadow.

Fescue, standing tall and proud, said to buttercup, 'Say you there, you are not welcome here.'

Buttercup, lying quite low and rather sheepish, replied, 'But I have no choice but to stay. I mean you no harm.'

Great Reedmace
Typha latifolia

Butterbur
Petasites hybridus

Spotted Orchid
Dactylorhiza fuchsii

Beauty and the bees: The flowers of the hillside provide food for the insects

17

'So untrue,' retorted Fescue. 'You are taking away my food source which I need to flourish and survive.'

'But there is acres to go around and you already have plenty,' said Buttercup timidly.

Fescue, stubborn in her way, wouldn't give any empathy. Instead she promptly ignored buttercup's plight and shouted 'Well we don't want you here. Be gone with you!'

Buttercup was so shocked and surprised by the actions of her cousin that all she could do was to politely bid her good day and keep her head down so as to not vex her anymore. Buttercup had faith that one day Fescue would eventually see sense and there would be some form of harmony within the meadow folk.

How right she was.

This manufacturing of pollen, carbon and genes are what's making the planet's breathing so much easier on Mother Earth. That leads me to explain that I have given the pretty things of this world like flowers a girl's image through the use of *her*, *she* or *brazen floozie* depending on their nature within the wild. You see, plants that have big blousy flowers are doing it for one reason, which is to attract and lure the insects of the planet. They put out their stall like a model would on a fashion world catwalk. The blokes also have their role in life. Not going down that route today though. The process called pollination aided by the humble bee is thus. Pollination is the process by which pollen is transferred to the female reproductive organs of a plant, enabling fertilisation to take place. All plants like all living things on the planet just want to pass on their seed to the next generation. In a roundabout way I have explained the birds and bees theory to anyone wishing to learn?

With a little bit of science over with, I return to the hillside with a relatively satisfied brain that I have covered most points early within this book. Like a comic book, pictures will be included so that I can squeeze a few more pages out. This is my second book – the novel, like nature, is a very slow process.

The hillside had indeed filled out, with most spaces filled with one variety of plant only. The winter served to even out the odds to the meadow's competitors. With a thick layer of snow and ice covering all of the hillside, it was hard to imagine in that mini ice age that life would ever return to the hill in spring. The plants on the other hand knew this cold situation very well and expected it to happen year in year out – it was a chance for them to hunker down and rest their roots until the spring. The insects found refuge within their hives or subterranean tunnels, and eggs were laid snugly in all available dry spaces within the hillside. The spring was to bring a new form of competitor into the field, a competitor like no other who would begin to change the shape of the hillside for many years to come.

Quercus awakens

Most of the planet's surface after the ice age was beginning to awaken from its slumber, and one such giant from the Jurassic period was the tree known as the mighty oak – its genetics created from the beech family of trees. The woodlands of southern Europe were on the march upwards and outwards and into Britain. They like the meadows were capitalising on the warming of their planet. The migration of plants and trees from the equatorial ring was painstakingly slow, and they were in no hurry to prove otherwise. This new kick start of life created by the spread of trees meant that all plant competitors had a tougher challenge ahead. Britain had also a huge contingent of wild beasts like deer, ox and wild boar, which would find refuge in these newly formed forests, the newly crowned giants of planet Earth. As animals took shape and form so did the humans of the world, and this race for supremacy went head to head with no particular species winning. In humans, the fine upstanding modern humans saw off their nearest competitors the Neanderthals, and eventually dominated them to the point of extinction in sub-Saharan Africa, an early sign of what was to be the blueprint in human history of war and conflict. To be fair though, modern man developed a stronger brain than his cousin; prejudice and racism were never really the issue here. The Neanderthals' seed was to continue in humans through future DNA tests so all was not lost anyway, but even in modern times Neanderthal is used as a derogatory term towards some. The trees like Quercus (the oak) grew up with all of the humans, and witnessed many come and go through their short life span. He studied them and missed them when they packed up and moved on, and he was only eventually greeted by similar humans as they followed the same nomadic path to glory. Quercus also witnessed that their species was getting larger. This turned a handful of humans into a small tribe, then eventually a small to large army. Humans' collective loyalty towards one another then created nations that would test other similar nations on their weaknesses and ideals. This was to start the fire that would smoulder for centuries to come.

Leaving the humans behind on the North African fringes means that we can return a few thousand years on when most of mainland Northern Europe was covered in dense woodland with the odd million square acres of meadows, lakes and snow-tipped mountains, a time when Britain had divided itself many millions years earlier from mainland Europe and the last boat was filled with plants, insects, animals plus the odd human. Quercus and his cousins found themselves stranded all alone on this newly formed island. It's not all so bad though – at least they can just get on with the things that matter like seed production and sunbathing? The meadows were waiting patiently for this big change, which I threatened them with some pages back. Time to put them out of their misery.

Now I'm not really quite sure how things truly came about over the coming years, all I know is that a slight twist of fate or a change in weather patterns can trigger a good or bad thing on our planet. Quercus was this twist of fate towards the meadow inhabitants. His seed had successfully spread independently over millions of years without any help from others. Front and centre stage came a herd of deer who were innocently rambling across fen and field, chewing and stomping all that had been provided to them from the plants. These animals are easily spooked due to their over-cautious nature towards humankind, and they are tainted with this curse purely as they are good meat and fair game or sport. They would naturally seek refuge within the relatively safe zones of a deep woodland or forest so as to maximise the deflection of a sharpened arrow heading in their direction. Their speed and agility gave them a great advantage over the crude accuracy of the early bows; sadly though without the trees for protection their odds are far slimmer. One such herd of deer – one stag with many does (lucky stag) – would be chased into deep woodland, the season being late summer–early autumn, with podgy wet ground on which many an acorn lay waiting for the next downpour to bury it deeper into the soil's substrate. Within a flash the stag leading the herd would unsuspectingly pick up an acorn within its hoof, and his frantic panic from a chasing predator would force him out of the wood into open ground. The stag set the pace for the herd for many, many miles until their stamina could take no more. This point of stop was of course, you guessed it, the meadow hilltop. Snorting and grunting followed from the exhausted herd, then they all realised that they had stopped in an area full of lush pasture at the foot

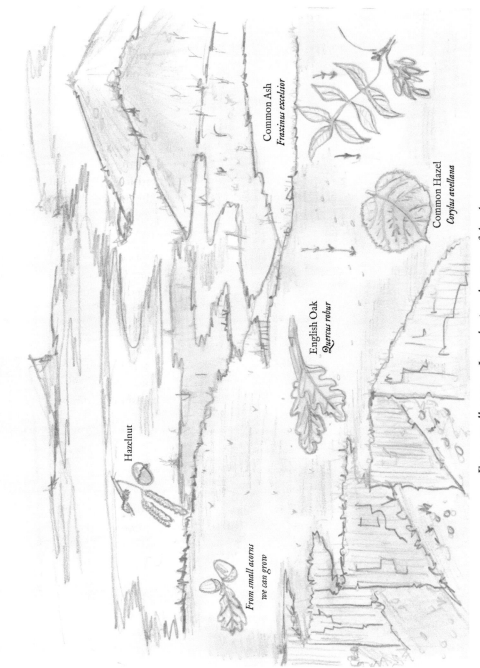

Common Ash
Fraxinus excelsior

Common Hazel
Corylus avellana

English Oak
Quercus robur

Hazelnut

*From small acorns
we can grow*

From small acorns: Introducing the stars of the show

of a commanding hill that overlooked a valley stretching for miles. Natural instincts followed after their heartbeats slowed, they turned to graze, and the meadow's plant inhabitants were then subjected to a barrage of constant stomp and chew from the deer for several days to come. Their location suited the herd perfectly as they continually patrolled the view and air for possible hunters.

The deer would also make good use of the pasture of grass and flowers to rest and sleep, squashing the ground into pockets of deer moulds. As they rested, the acorn lodged in the hoof of the stag would drop out due to the drying of his thick chunky-soiled hoof, and the stag would unsuspectingly start the beginning of a future woodland area. The does would also hold a similar seed type, with ash and hazel all within a few hundred metres of each other. Now I'm not saying that all woodlands are started in the same fashion across the planet, I just like to explore a particular scenario where animals, insects and indeed humans play a big part in the shaping of our landscape, be it a total coincidence or just sheer luck. The fact is that the landscape wasn't created by anyone in particular making any choice decisions about the best way forward. It just happened, and it is all around us. My fictional herd of deer connects all of its elements quite happily.

The time had eventually come when all the meadow plants were to accept that their planet was changing, and that the meadow was just one of those places. Fescue, buttercup and sorrel had lived with each other for years and slowly became more tolerant of their life together, but prejudices still ran deep from time to time. So when a common foe in the form of Quercus (oak), Fraxinus (ash) and Corylus (hazel) appeared, the plants all agreed to put aside their differences and create an alliance. This would begin a new chapter in the hillside's future.

The collective meadow plants began to experience slight changes within the soil structure and moisture. Happy in their own root structure and limitations, they put it down to less seasonal rainwater or the fact that they were not producing enough fodder within the ground due to an unseasonably late start from a late winter. The reality was that the three dominant native trees mentioned above – Quercus, Fraxinus and Corylus – were beginning to stretch out their roots at a very fast and alarming rate. Others would soon join this elite team of natives, but for the meantime let's stick with our three trees to the point when the meadow council had to make a collective decision about their future. Their plan was to surround the trees and try to stifle their growth through lack of light, moisture and nutrients.

The trees though had pre-empted their thoughts as they were already well below the meadow's soil substrate and into the leached pockets of nutrients within the shillet and rock substrate. The shrouding efforts of the meadow plants would only force the trees to bolt higher out of the meadow's limited height plus provide adequate moisture within their own roots on a hot summer's day. As the trees got taller they were able to produce more of their solar harvesters to soak up added food from above and below – their thickening girth gave them more reason to spread out thicker and stronger lateral roots anchored all together by a main tap root, and root hairs would then briskly seek out the valuable nutrients built up by the meadow's seasonal decay. Unlike their meadow cousins growing below them, the trees produced a larger mass of deciduous leaf that would smother the meadow folk and eventually feed the ground, and as the seasons moved on, the deposits grew thicker and more widespread. This would suppress any fresh re-growth of the meadow folk the next season, along with creating an ever-increasing shadow that would block out the plants' internal factory productions of food from the sun's rays.

Quercus was the first to seed and took full responsibility for his actions, and those of his future generations, within the meadow. The meadow had begun to accept his standing so an agreement was made to give each one some space in the name of 'nature's way'. They all agreed that it wasn't the first time that species had had to come to such an agreement, and it certainly wouldn't be the last. As they all breathed easily together over a midsummer night's clear sky they would look up at the stars and dream of similar such happenings on similar fortunate planets within our universe. Billions of years had given them all a common goal and purpose: to question their reason for being there in the first place. Fraxinus some 50 metres away had the same issues within his locale, with thankfully the same democratic answer amongst the plants. On the other hand Corylus, the pragmatic female, was subjected to a tougher time due to her stunted gene of height, and she would take some time to punch her way out of the meadow's stranglehold. Her genetics would initially force her leaf parallel to the ground, and she had to make do with mingling with the meadow plants as her fellow tree cousins grew taller and wider. Still, this taught her great patience and tolerance for her neighbours – a lesson that would serve her well in future years' growth. Corylus would be positioned between Quercus and Fraxinus as a kind of wise referee to the tantrums of her gutsy selfish cousins. The trees' maturity would also give them the valuable life skill of tolerance over the many full seasons of life.

I choose to leave the meadow with its newly embedded immigrants alone for a while, just to keep you up to speed with the other up and coming species on the planet.

Humanity's revolution

Humankind's pace was like Quercus and co, although their need to grow strong and masterful taught them only hatred and selfishness towards their fellow species. The Neanderthal species had all but gone from the face of the planet, but their gene was nonetheless present in future seeds of humankind. Now did this give us a race of both brainy and thick people or is it our parents' guidance and ambitions that make us clever or savvy? I sit on the fence on this one as I write this book, for I'm self-taught, no one pushed me to do my sums and my alphabet. I just got on with it – like the plants of the world I just did what came naturally to me. I'm not wishing I was a top scientist or brain surgeon, but they all need a plumber to fix that tap and a builder to build their house. We all have unique skills and jobs to do in the world to keep the planet ticking.

A bit more local to our green and pleasant isle were the Mesolithic cave dwellers of pre-history. They hopped over and stayed in the UK sometime between the thaw and the odd land-shifting earthquake. Probably about 10,000 years ago, so let's just say 'a long, long time ago' in a fairy tale voice. It was no idyllic fairy tale for the humans though, living in damp caves full of stalagmites and stalactites. Their technological advancement was at this point stone flint, fire and fashionable mammoth or sabre tooth tiger gowns all neatly coupled with a strong leather belt, oh and don't forget the early Ugg-like boot; no socks or pants though, tough humans they were then. These early humans were hunter-gatherers, a skill passed down through many evolutionary ancestors who took to the taste of meat rather than the veggie diet of plants, and they began to control their local area in packs or tribes. These athletic, fast humans had great stamina to chase prey over many miles before unleashing their projectiles of spears to kill their prey in one fell swoop. The unfortunate animal would not only feed a small tribe, but also its bones would make the early jewellery and hand tools to better the tribe's simple lives. When humans developed the art of the bow the chase became less demanding on their bodies, and this would enable humans to begin to think more cleverly. It wasn't too long before they were out of their damp caves and on the open plains, living in simple round-houses of stone and wood. The tribes of Britain, albeit small at first, were about to make their mark on their surrounding landscape as did the tribes of the world. A simple, relatively civilised turning point for all the tribes of the northern hemisphere had begun to appear.

Their increasing population would be at first sustainable within the environment they all shared. Their needs were simple as they built simple homes to suit their simple existence. Warring tribes would find peace one way or the other, despite the ancient Druids passing blame on them for bad weather patterns or a stillborn child. It was this scaremongering that would lead the early humans to fear the moon, the odd solar eclipse would really freak them out, and their understanding of all this would take a little more science and brain power. Paganism would also fuel their afterlife beliefs due to their ignorance of the universe, something the plants had worked out and mulled over for centuries. Humankind was gifted a combination of brilliant ingenious genes from the amalgamation of many chemicals in their favour, but they really didn't know this and took it all for granted. So as the plants, trees and organisms of Britain were advanced enough already to compute this, then as a being they were willing for us humans to catch up, like the less advanced child in the class.

Farmers

I suppose it was inevitable that humans would discover simple farming methods, purely through the need to control their stock of yak or ox – they didn't want their cattle to roam freely, as they were used to, from meadow to meadow just so that a neighbouring tribe could claim them for their own. The poor ox for many thousands of years roamed Britain in herds chewing, stomping and breeding on the run. Their nomadic graze would take them from meadow to stream to hilltop and beach without any restraints or rule. They probably had unknowingly passed through our hilltop meadow from time to time. They were strong and bullish in their nature towards any predator wishing to make steak of them; like the deer, wild boar and badger they were cousins of a prehistoric mammal that pulled itself out of the ice age to be who it is today. Who knows what the next million years will produce?

Humans on the other hand had other plans for their evolutionary path, or is it just nature playing out its course? The newly named farmers of the planet would control and confine these animals in large stockades of wood. Finally, after years of submission, the cattle got used to their human masters and bowed down to their needs. This meant they lost their nomadic wild lifestyle and became controlled, dumber beasts. They began to rely on the humans to give them fresh pasture plus water, and they began to not think for themselves, living, breeding and dying in a field not of their choice but of humans'. I'm not saying this is such a bad thing as I tuck into my regular Sunday roast – it was just how things panned out on the big scale of things. As the herds got bigger though, so did the humans, and as they gorged on a rich meat diet so did their waistlines, from Neolithic athleticism to podgy red-faced farmer within a couple of centuries. Laziness though can also prompt invention to make your life easier, so weaponry and farming implements came about from the humans' additional spare time. They need not hunt for their food anymore as it was already on their doorstep, and the thrill of the chase was slowly replaced by the amble ramble across a grazing stock. These practices, strangely learnt from foreign tribes of the Middle East (Syria to be exact) took a couple of thousand years to be fully embraced on our fair isle.

It wasn't too long before land was sectioned off for crops like barley and wheat, and strange woolly creatures called sheep and goats would be introduced from mainland Europe, whereas the humble pig was domesticated from the native wild boar. You can imagine the impact this had on the land – woodlands felled to be cleared for grazing, and once exhausted then ploughed up by the servant ox to plant crops. It wasn't all too bad though, because the local wildlife had more open fields to choose from as the woodland areas were cleared. Rabbits and deer had a population boom and the fox had a stable diet to feast on, not to mention when the chickens arrived. There were winners and losers though, with the percentage share still at this point in favour of the plants and trees. Safety in numbers ensured that they could continue their day to day life unaffected by what was going on around them. The plants and trees were just happy to be of service to humankind as they had been with each other for the past odd million years.

New age of farming

The British landscape began to slowly change, although this was not noticed by the humans. As the plough and ox began to tear and rip the ground, the trees would stealthily make a move upwards and outwards. The heathland and open hillside normally reserved for gorse and heather would be nudged out by the trees, whereas the heavy woodlands of the lower lands would be replaced by grass and wheat, all in a very topsy turvy way. Rich deposits of unmanaged bracken and grass would make an ideal seeding bed for the evicted trees, for as they were to be moved by humans for their progression, so the trees needed their space to do likewise. The open hillside also provided great vantage points for the warring tribes to secure and protect themselves from pillaging pikes and marauders – they really needed the highest hills to survey their fields of wheat and cattle to repel such invaders of their land. A large smelly tribe with the intention of mayhem and misery towards a hill fort is best observed from high and afar, but as humans get cleverer they come to realise it's a lot of hard work to battle and climb a steep hill without any chance of success. Perhaps their fitter Neolithic ancestors would have taken it on due to their athletic physique? A modern-day chancer would probably say 'Stuff that for a game of soldiers' and move on to less fortunate villagers down the road.

These natural geographically squeezed land masses were also ideal for building ramparts and ditches to bolster a tribe's defences, plus wear down the unfittest invader and force them to give up any dreams of glory. So as the wooden ramparts were constructed, so naturally any perimeter trees and plants would be cleared, chopped and dug up to create an impregnable hill fort, housing all the tribe's grain pits and cattle when trouble turned up. So easy to chuck a spear, boulder and arrow downhill at your enemy rather than hurling anything upwards, well at least until weaponry got to the stage of the catapult – now there's a great way of hitting them where it hurts. The trees obliged the humans, seeing this as a chance to be useful to them as they did amongst the plants around them. They realised that if they were to accommodate the humans' needs then the humans would be less harsh in future years, creating a sustainable symbiotic existence between the two gene pools, well at least for a while anyway. All the trees needed was the chance to carry on their seed for future generations. What harm could come from allowing the humans the odd acre every now and then?

This aptly makes me return to the hillside where the battle of Quercus and co versus the meadow was truly being won by the trees on the northern banks of the hillside. The trees had gained valuable height and width over the past 100 years – sorry, it's so easy to skip loads of seasons for the benefit of the story (a bit boring if I gave a week by week account of their progress; a bit like watching paint dry). Quercus, Fraxinus and Corylus were by no means boring to me. Just like all good friends it's best to meet them regularly over the year to catch up on fresh news and gossip – you only get fed up with each other if around them for too long. The trees took the same principles on board, and their distance apart from each other meant they all had the freedom to explore their ground in their own time. Most of their busy life was navigating their tap roots into the rock as straight as possible to give equal anchorage for the lateral roots to spread horizontally. What happens below ground matters above ground for all the trees, and this underground effort enabled them all to ignore each other for long periods throughout the winters, only to push upwards and outwards in the spring and summer to show off their unique solar harvesters. It is at this point that they can relax and discuss together their progress and problems of the last six months. This conversation is heightened and enjoyed the most on the eve of the summer solstice, as it is for the humans on Salisbury Plain. You can hear it when there is light rain in the air accompanied by a small breeze – the leaves appear to clap to one another, congratulating each other for all the hard work over the last 12 months. Words like bravo and top ho, well in tree language anyway.

Quercus would boast the most to Fraxinus about his biggest achievements and strengths to date, Fraxinus would boast about his fast growth and seed dispersal, and Corylus stuck in the middle would act as the referee and remind them it's not all about size, it's what you do with it that matters. Enough said there then. Shrouded in their own self-importance, they ignored what they had heard on the tree grapevine about the increasing human population around them. Their hilltop, like most of the commanding vantage points along the channel and moors, would soon be earmarked for settlement. The meadow hilltop was naturally rocky and steep on all but one side, and this north side home to our friends the trees would serve to house the humans' temporary workshops and cattle stockades. However, the trees' spot midway up the hill luckily escaped from a massive tribe of humans who capitalised on the hilltop location to build a stronghold to spy on and overlook a similar tribe near the coastal areas some miles away to the west. These tribes had fallen out over the land rights of the boggy moorland that kept them apart. They were both splinter groups from the tribes to the north, where a great gorge met the sea. Brizzle I think they called it?

The hillside tribe nonetheless was keen to command this wet boggy moorland to hopefully sometime lay siege to their northern cousins and claim back their heritage. They laughed between them, saying things like 'It may be wet and boggy but it's our wet and boggy land – let no one take it from us.' Turned out though that the hillside went from temporary to permanent to the tribe as they all warmed to their surroundings, and this made them appreciate the land and trees around them, rather than destroying them. At first Quercus and Fraxinus served to define the play areas for the hill fort children, who would play out mock battles with wooden swords between the two great trees. The kids' mission was to protect their designated tree from destruction by their fellow invader. Corylus was naturally left in the middle and generally stepped over or used as shelter from rocks and sticks lobbed towards each kiddy camp. Naturally the trees were left intact to enable future battles to take place, perhaps with the odd whipped leaf or branch to symbolise the winning team. This childhood play protected the trees from future removal, and as the child turned warrior the trees' future was assured as a mark of respect by their children and their children's children. Quercus and Fraxinus would sometimes think back to their early days as young saplings with great joy.

Although most of the meadow plants like the grasses and sorrel were uprooted and moved to create mounds, they bounced back strong as ever to carpet the hill once again and to claim their place on their ancient hillside. In rare, peaceful times cattle were allowed to roam free around the ramparts, and this familiar seasonal action was pleasing to the fescues, sorrel and buttercup. The cattle would still poach, poo and stomp, but hey the plants were used to it. In the lean periods of drought and in the dry conditions of the summer months the ground lay flat, giving just enough room and time for the self heal, clover and daisy to pop up. This provided the insects with a valuable food source, and when all was randomly abandoned by human and cattle alike, their movement would then pollinate the late crops of wheat and barley for the harvest and the following winter's supply. So you see, the balance was happily reset after so much upheaval. The meadows in the foreground would also show signs of early retirement into the ground as the sun baked their seed heads and swords, and a wandering wolf pack would take up residence until seen off by the angry humans – their relationship and friendship would take some time to establish. When wolf was eventually bred into hound and dog, man's best friend would then help humans to control cattle in a symbiotic language of whistles and bleeps.

Humans were beginning to be innovative with the resources around them, as after so many years tucked away in caves they had seen a new lease of life. They began to understand the workings of the plants and trees for their own benefit, and things like coppicing and pollarding became a regular day to day task as they understood the trees' growth habits and strengths. The humans could reduce a small tree like a hazel down to a stumpy height knowing that she would regrow and regenerate in future years, and this sustainable action would provide them with kindle and poles for hurdles and fencing without having to lose the tree and seek further afield. Using local resources saved them a lot of walking. Corylus was keen to oblige, knowing that her future was saved from uprooting and clearance for crops or cattle, and she regularly told Quercus and Fraxinus of her importance to the humans in a sarcastic way.

Quercus was pleased for Corylus after the many years of guilt and taking pity on her due to her small stature within the woodland copse on the hillside. Little did Quercus know that his legend as a tree within Britain had earned him a pagan respect and he'd become a symbol of all that was good amongst the tribes of this fair isle – but best not give him too much of an ego, hey. Fraxinus on the other hand saw his seed grow fast within the catchment of his canopy and beyond, and the humans capitalised on this for quick turnaround of firewood and kindling. All a bit annoying for him at first, but they seemed to only take what they needed and let him be within his friends, his height and girth seeming too much like hard work for the ever so slow, lazy humans around him.

Humans began to realise the importance of their surroundings through a baby's eye mentality. Unlike the plants and trees around them, the universe held so many questions to them, and their guesswork and their quest for understanding led to a new era of thinkers on the planet's history. I'm going to take you back within a time zone parallel to the hillside's history to the equatorial and tropic zones of the planet which were humans' cradle of evolution. We have learnt of great civilisations like the Egyptians who worshipped the sun god Ra. Their quest for understanding of the universe, in particular the immortal stars in the sky, led them to build the great pyramids. The then tribal leaders called pharaohs were worshipped through many thousands of years by their devoted subjects. The pharaohs' initial vision that the afterlife was somewhere hidden in the stars gave hope to all the slaves and workers who died and suffered for them. These pharaohs were just clever humans who saw an opportunity to create a notion that they were super human or gods themselves, and to defy their ideals meant death or banishment to the infertile wilderness. But wow, what they gave to humankind in the form of technology and human advancement was the beginning of many other great civilisations being formed in their wake. All we see about that great civilisation is the pyramids and a lot of sand, making us wonder how they survived in such a barren environment. The truth is the Sahara was initially fertile, when first formed by the thaw of the ice age, so the answer may indeed be found in the history of many other planets before ours. Later, as the Sahara became hotter and drier, humans just moved north or south to avoid the heat and took up residence in a greener and more fertile land for their own tribes' future security. The Mediterranean was the next area to breed future greats of humans, born from the histories of many great humans before them. Their technology was just passed down to the next user who would make it work better and more efficiently for their own end. The hillside tribes of Britain were unaware that their cousins were far more advanced than them, probably down to the weather being better down south, giving them more time to mull over ideas in the sun rather than worrying about keeping dry or warm in a typical British climate.

Well that's my thoughts anyway.

Rising civilisations

Humankind's ebb and flow of rule over the planet meant that other great civilisations were being created every thousand years. The thinkers of the Greek empire were one such civilisation.

They, like the Egyptian tribes before them, languished in the warm summers and relatively mild winters. This gave them ample time to think and dream about their night sky. Their thinking created a mystical world of gods in the heavens that oversaw their own personal destinies. This thinking created characters that best suited the planets, regions or human traits, like Zeus, God of the sky, Poseidon, God of the sea, Demeter, God of agriculture, and so on. Many more were initially dreamed up, and then, after the creation of so many myths and a few strange happenings (normally after a night on the lash) the gods became believable amongst the humans. This human superstition was to be replicated the world over, born out of ignorance of our universe. It seemed the easy option to blame an imaginary god when there was a flood or a plague of locusts. Now I'm not wishing to upset all you religious types but we have had and still have many gods from many nations, all claiming theirs is the best. The plants on the other hand had already embraced science and understanding long before we were out of the primordial soup. Humans would only make a plant or tree a god of their own when the mood took them – good for the plant as it established a relatively secure future.

It's funny though how thinking or dreaming of something totally unreal can make you discover other things and inventions. I myself was allowed to scribble and doodle on my bedroom wall like the cavemen before me. This allowed me to unassumingly become an artist some years later. The Greek people had their flaws but also created great thinkers like Socrates, Plato and Aristotle. Science was born from the stargazers and the laidback lifestyles of such a clever race. Their teachings would kickstart an age of discovery, and they would question our reason for being, along with all that's good and bad in the world. Humans had developed a conscience, but still felt the need to conquer. This brings me to a couple of mythical lads called Romulus and Remus in a land not so distant from Greece called Italy (specifically Rome) in today's understanding. These two lads were the love children of a god, abandoned at first but saved by a she-wolf and a wood-pecker on the banks of the river Tiber. It's a far-fetched story but, hey, not so mad amongst all the other gods in the world. They were both found by a shepherd who brought them up to form the Roman Empire, which went on to become one of the world's biggest conquerors. In reality, a group of tribes that got together learnt from others and created a massive army built on knowledge and very tall blokes who kicked ass all along the Med area. The god thing gave them belief and reason to pillage from other such tribes and persuade those tribes that the Roman way was the best way, telling the tribes that their God was inferior to the Roman god, who must be obeyed!

Time has taught us, though, that through any military advancement humankind has flourished, purely because the need to conquer created a better, more efficient killing machine. These advances gave humans better tools and skills to put to use elsewhere, like in agriculture and construction. The Greeks had already given them laws of physics and maths to help create aqueducts and catapults, and the Egyptian tribes had provided them with grain and gold. All this ended up creating commerce, trade and money, which was universally pleasing to the likes of humankind as they began to have status and possessions. Future leaders would then be more competitive and backstabbing towards each other, leading to murder and deception.

Still no change there then!

The plants of the world at this point of humankind's enlightenment were just happy to hitch a ride to the next village or country, happy to be passed around, shared and eaten in all manner of ways. Their road trip was further extended through tribes' movement outwards from the Sahara to the temperate zones of the Med and northern Europe. This untimely migration was at first a shock to all those plants moved from their native surroundings.

The weather was similar but less hot, so they just made hay when the sun shined and adapted as they naturally had done from century to century. Along with dried herbs, grains of wheat were the first to move, providing valuable carbs for the marching armies. Most perishable crops like tomato would take some adjusting to cooler climates, hence the slow development of pizza within the European countries. Vines for wine surprisingly adapted to the cool temperatures well but needed a hot summer to ripen fully, so mead it was for the Britons for the while. All these plants, with the mixture of the odd olive and lemon tree, were introduced but failed dismally under a carpet of snow or ice. It would take a step upwards in glasshouses for them to flourish. Northern Europe, like our home hillside, would harness a glut of protein through deer and boar which would certainly sustain many a tribe for a long period until their settlements caught up with creating a stable crop.

First to fall to the Romans were the French tribes. The Germanic tribes were less willing to play game and battled hard until they eventually gave in to Roman wit and weaponry. These Saxons would have to bide their time to experience glory once again. Britain was last to fall, primarily as it took a more logistical approach due to the fast currents of the channel, but the Romans succeed not only in conquering the land but also the sea in the form of man-propelled galleys. These red cedar-hulled ships melded with iron and dowel were big enough and tough enough to carry large legions plus withstand the sea's wrath, and this gave the Romans an added advantage when landing on the shallow shores of old Kent.

They came prepared for the long stay, their boats packed with tents and grain, dried herbs plus an added bonus of strength and height against their foe. You see the Romans like the Greeks had a history of competitive competitions that made them a strong race – the Olympian legacy was born from the Med where humans pitched themselves against each other in games of mental and physical power. Admittedly it was all egos and testosterone to be the best Godlike creation humankind can muster, but all in all a good healthy battle to sharpen wits and tactics against a less worthy opponent in war. Not really good news for the defending tribes of Britain as they were totally unaware of what was afoot on the coasts of Dover and beyond. Still, it was inevitable that someone would eventually turn up and spoil the barbecue.

Just to accelerate this a little bit more, we knew the outcome of the invasion of AD43 when the Romans kicked our ass and settled with little or no resistance save some woman on a chariot from the northern tribe. Like all things happening in the Home Counties region it took a few years to reach the back of beyond of the south west, purely due to the Welsh and Cornish refusing any let up in their defences, along with the Scots in the north. The Romans settled in all the best places and chipped away at their enemies as part of their job description. Sadly though, our peaceful tribe on the hilltop back home was to have a rude awakening.

How many years did it take for our native tribe to build that hill fort, only for a well organised advanced tribe to knock it down in weeks. It's not as if they weren't prepared, as the invaders' galleys could be seen from the coastal hill forts for weeks on end travelling up the gorge to Brizzle. Hill forts like Maiden Castle in Dorset put up a good fight but were eventually starved out by the surrounding dug-in legions.

Here's my possible series of events leading up to the fall of the hilltop tribe. Three quarters of the hill fort was perched on a high rock face that overlooked the flooded estuary, not an ideal place for a marching army with the odd catapult to haul their weaponry across – far too boggy. They probably came from the north east, being that Bristol was their base, and took the less steep but steady gradient, as their roads were built in straight lines so the legions naturally followed its path. They did this to see what was in front of them without any corners for a tribe of mad British pikes to hide round and attack them. Once positioned they were able to scout around and see that on the east side of the hill was the gate house, the logical place for the yokels to haul food and water from. Camped out on the neighbouring higher ground close enough to worry the tribe, but far enough away to avoid any arrows, they sent out a few sorties to test the tribe's weaknesses over consecutive weeks, then bided their time, at least until the hill tribe got restless and started throwing stones and spears at regular patrols. Then the Romans probably unleashed hell on them one early morning, when the majority were sleeping off a hangover after a night on the lash. The Romans were of course sober and organised?

Fed up with the hassle of the dogged Romans, the tribe admitted defeat and accepted jobs as 'walkers'. This brings me to the point of explaining my surname, a job title that was defined by the Romans. A 'walker' would stamp out grapes or carry out laundry duties by stamping out cloth in a bucket full of … No, you don't need to know. Got out the stains well in socks and undergarments though!

New tenants

Quercus, Fraxinus and Corylus along with all of the meadow team were amazed at the efficiency of their new uninvited landlords, whose scale armour and shields resembled a giant armadillo, especially as most of the high-tech carts and catapults were made up with their tree cousins from far afield. Such workmanship and care given to the creation of their wooden implements made the trees think, 'Eh up, this is not so bad.' They felt needed again, albeit by a different tribe. It wasn't too long before the hill fort was totally abandoned and left to rack and ruin, only to be replaced by a Roman building nearby. An eerie silence fell upon the hill, as the arguing tribesmen and children playing were replaced by the ghost wind and the birds cackling in the trees. A kestrel hovered over the hill in search of field mice, and above her was the circling telescopic eye of a buzzard. The Roman temple was completed, and the trees were amazed by the speed and efficiency of its construction. Granted, most of the labour was provided by the conquered locals under pain of death or torture, but that's the human way. The trees took pity on the humans all the same and questioned why they just couldn't all get on like us, for without help and unity you are just one simple tree in the middle of a field of loneliness. Humans would take a long time to realise that they are not superior over one another, and they are part of nature and nature is part of them. Until that time they would develop more ways to outwit and conquer other humans until there was nothing else to do.

The pace of the trees' growth couldn't compete with the pace of human progress, but this is where I question their development. How are we to know that a plant or tree is rushing its growth from seed to full height? It may be as much in a hurry as us or as slow as a snail in pace – laid back or totally stressed to produce first flower then seed, eventually to collapse and have a holiday afterwards. How do we know whether a plant's engine of growth is geared in first or fifth gear? Only a time lapse camera will speed it up or slow it down for our amusement. From space though we are all moving at an incredibly high speed, given our planet's spin through our solar system, something we can't comprehend while sitting down, and it would make us very dizzy if we all tried to stop and stare.

The plants embrace this every day. As the Earth tracks the sun's arc from east to west, they need no sunglasses or shades to embrace the glare and heat of this celestial body, they only need to fan out and worship their life blood as if with stretched out hands. As the wind pulls them to and fro they rigidly strain to hold their ground facing towards the sun's rays, and some, like the fescues on the meadow, just seem to go with it, and relax to enjoy the ride. The amazing thing is when then dry they appear so fragile to touch making it seem impossible for their tubular frame to withstand so much abuse from the elements. Like a magician's sleight of hand they hold their secrets up their sleeves, and it's up to us to try and learn from their magic and then put it to good use on things that really matter in life. Their movement in the wind seen from afar is a glory to see as the moon and wind wave their hands creating a sea of movement and flow. Imagine if that picture of flow was seen from space. Now that would make you truly dizzy.

You see the Romans were superstitious beings and believed that after every conquest they should try to embrace the local myths and legends so as not to upset their own gods in the sky. Bad luck and good fortune were of their own device, hence why they built a temple to ease their conscience and make their life more bearable. They heard stories of the mighty oak being a symbol of strength for the tribes plus the importance of the other materials around them, and it is through this that our friends were once again saved from the sharpened axe. This made Quercus grateful to the Romans, but it wasn't so for their cousins of other species situated on the hills, plateau and surrounding areas. The flooded marshland was safe from development, well at least for a while anyway. This was home to the willow, willow herb and welted thistle, only too happy to spread their fluffy seeds all along the stream's edge when the wind blew. These would reach the outer perimeters of the hillside meadow in wet summers, only to be bashed and trampled by the grazing cattle. A picture of colour it was at full tilt in the summer though, with its pinks, reds and greens, a nuisance to no one except the cattle and grazers of the meadows, to whom they were inedible. Giving a valuable food source for the butterfly and bee when all is exhausted elsewhere, these plants like the fescues and sorrel would intermix and weave amongst each other, all daring to be as close to the water's edge as possible. The willow would command the landscape – like the plants he would hug the water's edge and anchor his roots within the moist silty river deposits. The odd meander of the stream would limit his growth but the river was as deep as it was wide. His soft wood would sometimes split under the weight of his own solar harvesters, but the benefit from this sudden loss of limb was to the beaver's dam further downstream, providing fortune to its family of kits. The wood was also utilised by humans, as when a willow had had its fill it would give out, leaving a hollow husk, and an opportunist clever tribesman would create a small boat or canoe and brag to his friends of his newly found vessel. For sure they all wanted one from that point onwards but kept a few hundred willows going so that future boatmen could enjoy messing about on the water. Well, it's better than walking anyway. The Romans had no use for the previous tribes' toys as they had a bigger toy to take them further up channel. The willow's other benefit to humans would take many hundreds of years to be realised, easing the pain of hangover or body ache in the form of aspirin.

A peaceful period of time was enjoyed by all on the hilltop, and their natural cycles were unhindered for years. The Romans brought stability between the warring tribes, so with no enemy to test them they began to integrate as Anglo-Roman people. Quercus and friends would be left to spread their seed much further afield in a randomly shambolic way, humans far gone save the odd traveller or Roman priest, and letting nature do its thing on the hillside. The trees' roots would continue to rip through the ground and their leaves would continue to create a higher canopy of shade over the ground. Give them a hundred years and they would all be connecting back together as if nothing had really happened. The trees on the hilltop, like all woodlands in the area, had pushed out the meadow plants in a slow eviction southward; ivy and fern plus bluebell had migrated north from the west, weaving and matting under the tree canopies. They all enjoyed the healthy thick leaf mould the trees provided them with. Quercus at this point stood really tall and proud over these small plants. He would peer downwards and muse over what they were saying to each other. Corylus on the other hand was busy being occupied by some new tenants in her once coppiced trunk, now covered in a blanket of trapped twigs and leaf mould – a family of dormice had taken up residence. Corylus felt like a surrogate mum to them all, feeding them with nuts in the spring to summer then bedding them down in the winter for hibernation. She really didn't mind her seed being eaten as the competition from her relatives around her needed thinning out now and again so that she could breathe a little into the ground. She had enough problems keeping Quercus and Fraxinus at bay. Quercus was noticing though that although it was nice to have the ground shaded by the ground cover plants like ivy in the summer, they had a habit of eventually climbing up to the very top of a tree to produce their flower and seed. He was prepared to tolerate ivy, so long as it was kept in check. He thought it was best to have a word.

Quercus was a mild mannered tree who spoke with a booming bass voice. He asked the ivy, 'Would you mind awfully not being so persistent in your growth habit? It's proving to be quite a bore. You see the trees really don't want this new garment over them and it's beginning to get a bit tight around their canopies and starting to choke them slightly.'

Naturally the ivy though was having none of it and ignored his plea to give everyone some space, which only caused more friction amongst the forest community. Quercus also noticed the ivy kicking his heels at this base of his trunk, and unable to defend himself his fate was in the lap of the gods or indeed the universe. By chance, some seasons before this point in time, a family of red squirrels had been rudely evicted from the pine forest to make way for human structures, and they had all sought refuge in the nearest free woodland on the hill beside the boggy plain. Quercus had lost a limb some seasons previously thanks to a cruel wind, and this had created an open chasm in his trunk, first occupied by a woodpecker which had fled from a flock of troublesome magpies. So a vacancy for the tenancy of the gap was filled by the squirrels. Perfect. Although Quercus's nut was a bit heavy for the red squirrel, he enjoyed Corylus's seed more but didn't want to offend his landlord's kind nature, so his family chewed slowly when times were lean in the winter. My point is the squirrels had very sharp claws with which they acrobatically clung around the tree's tough bark exterior, and this is where the ivy's soft tissue of leaf and stem would fall foul of their constant ramblings up and down Quercus. It wasn't long before the ivy gave up and looked elsewhere and concentrated its effort on a less fortunate victim nearby. Quercus was sorry it had come to this but what with diplomacy failing badly, more stringent action was needed to resolve the situation. He heard through the woodland canopy that the ivy was happy and well on the rocky slopes of the abandoned hill fort, so all's well that ends well there then.

The fern on the other hand is as old as the planet itself. My god they tell us a tale or two about the history of life on Earth, having rubbed shoulders with the dinosaurs, been through the adolescent growing pains of the planet, and seen the evolution of humankind. Wow, they're like time machines all wrapped up in their beautifully-curled fronds, some locked in fossils with the dinosaurs, others growing well in present time. Thousands of varieties there are, all looking strikingly similar to one another. Our woodland fern is named hart's tongue. This ancient survivor loves the calcareous substrate of limestone and clay, and its survival and reproduction mechanism is contained in its spores under its fronds, which are both male and female. These are released on the wind and settle in moist ground, where they mix together and produce a plant, totally unaided by insects or humans. To live this solitary free life has enabled this fern to get on with things through some really tough times in the planet's history. It also benefits the soil's pH when it breaks down and decays into the ground, which on a woodland scale is really good for all. Quercus felt compelled to learn more from his common ancestor so as to broaden his knowledge of the environment around him, so he set out to listen better, closer to the ground, with fresh uncoppiced branches so he and the fern could interact better. This would be the start of a great bond between the fern and the oak, like two old fogies reminiscing over past times in a comfortable armchair – you know, pipe and slipper scenario. Ahh, those were the days.

What Quercus learnt from the fern that day was that they were all con-nected together underground in a unique wood-wide web of fungi that sent messages to them all in times of stress and hardship, along with joy and happiness, all in a symbiotic kind of social media way. Quercus knew of this but he couldn't connect to it with any form of reasoning until now. Perhaps humans will have the potential to understand this in time and help unlock their own hidden secrets from deep within their brains or indeed their souls? Quercus embraced this whole new sensation but chose not to fully connect with the whole science thing. The fern then went on to explain that they had all heard his screams of pain when the lightning strike ripped off one of his limbs, and that those who chose to embrace it felt great sympathy for him. 'Quercus, you are not alone within the wood,' the fern said. Quercus was comforted by this and was happy to hear that he didn't suffer in silence. He vowed to offer similar empathy to others endur-ing such an unforeseen tragedy in the future.

The little folk

Another welcomed woodland plant was the native bluebell, accompa-nied by the ramsons or wild garlic, both carried on the wind from the southern forests of Britain. They both took advantage of the trees' pockets of nitrogen and leaf mould in the ground, as their small bead-like seeds would easily penetrate a blanket of dogged ivy and germinate within the rich layers of topsoil. These early bulbous plants would make good use of the ample light levels within the forest floor when spring was in its infancy, appearing when the canopy was at its translucent stage of growth. Fraxinus was first to see them appear as they snuggled into his heavy deposits of leaf mould. He noticed though that both bluebell and wild garlic were growing as if one, similar to the meadow plants of sorrel and buttercup. He observed this miniature battle of supremacy with great interest. They seemed to get along well but the competition was fierce as they made fast headway. The allium, though, liked the higher bank rather than the bluebell's habit of heading down slope, and a sweet smell of garlic then perfumed the woodland air before flowers from both parties appeared. This was to mark the beginning of the spring growth for all the woodland community, when the amazing carpet of blue and white festooned the floor in waves of shambolic tapestry. The bluebell and wild garlic then surprisingly congratulated each other, which took Corylus and co by surprise – they all thought they were bitter rivals but it was just a ruse to trick the trees into thinking they didn't get on. 'Got ya!' they laughed.

Their circle of life would slowly fade away as the sun crept higher into the sky. First to fade would be their leaf, as all energy was put into flower then seed, before they waved goodbye to the trees and fell asleep into the ground. Corylus was saddened by the departure of the little devils but looked forward to their arrival next season when their performance would be put on for any new saplings and plants on the woodland floor. Seed heads of the bluebells stayed as a reminder of their glory for many months to come; the allium was less obvious to see but rest assured they were both alive and kicking below. Fraxinus noticed though that when the trees' trunks and branches took on a naked frame in the winter, the seed heads in the meadow stayed put all the way up to when their regrowth appeared in the spring. It's as if they stayed just long enough to remind themselves that life goes on regardless of when all energy has been spent. He also noticed that humankind preferred to bury their dead husks in the ground; they then placed fresh flowers on the grave annually as a matter of respect. Strange, he thought, but then it's nice to see that plants are chosen to show respect to the human dead. When the hillside tribe was defeated all was lost, but hey, some great fresh daisies were pushed up where they lay.

The Romans brought many beliefs with them on their long journey from the Mediterranean, along with many different plants that were native to home, helping them with their home comforts and diet. The native tribes of Britain had similar plants but none as exotic as the grape vine or lavender bush. The native plants attracted pollinators that were similar to the insects abroad, which made the transition to a cooler climate bearable to the Mediterranean plants – after all, the Med also can experience the odd downpour and snow in the course of a full year. The one thing that Britain lacked then, as it does now, was continual warmth and sunshine, which really cheesed off the conquering Romans. They tolerated all this due to the rich fertile soil for growing wheat and corn, crops which were provided by the natives' sweat and toil over many years. Their imported plants took well to the ground even though their path of discovery had been so rapid, as it had been for the plants that had been moved from the Nile delta to the Med through previous human advancements. It was a new land rich in the resources of tin and wood, oh and a new-found spa in the south west in which to bathe the true Roman way.

The plants of Britain by this time had seen many comings and goings, so the new introduction of a foreign invader was not such a bad thing. One such plant, the lavender, charmed her way in with her sweet perfume that only served to soothe and freshen the air. The insects were naturally enticed by her lure and drank her sweet nectar in the heat of the midday sun. When lavender and oregano were singing, the whole wide hillside would sit and listen. Ah, they all said to themselves, this is what summer is all about.

The Romans provided us with hypocaust, road and wine along with a reasonably good diet of food when offered the scraps from the table. Strangely, though, despite living here for four hundred-odd years, the Romans didn't leave behind their Latin plant names, which only appeared in English several hundred years later. The plants were happy with any names, but they liked the Latin ones as they gave them additional credibility. For instance, I have chosen to name the trees in the Latin purely as it sounds better than our common word. Well it makes me look educated anyway!

The poor old vine though took some time to adjust and its wine never really tasted the same as the Italian or French bottle of plonk, but as the locals didn't know anything different it all tasted fab with a bit of yeast and soft fruit. Zider from the south west had a bigger following with the alcoholic farmers though. Well you can't make a good Cheddar from the slopes of the Dordogne or Sicily can you? It's all the cattle and fine pasture of Britain that gives our Cheddar that strong taste.

The Romans like previous civilisations also brought over many medical and herbal skills to our shores. They, like the ancient Babylonians and Egyptians, founded the early practices of the apothecary. They harnessed the healing powers of many plants to aid such human weaknesses as constipation through aloe vera, of which our native sorrel has the same attribute. Certain mints can help alleviate sores, along with the additional oil-based

41

herbs like lavender that have relaxing and soothing healing powers. The plants of the world were beginning to be recognised by humankind as their weaknesses appeared from century to century. The human gene was beginning to be stretched further afield, which made their bodies weak as their population grew. The plants and trees stayed relatively the same, give or take the odd cross pollination from the insects forming a new colour or variety, so they held strong as a living organism – they had no big plans or ambition. They were only too pleased to help the humans in any way they could, given their natural connection to humanity over billions of years.

The British tribes had also embraced a small amount of the healing powers of plants but lacked the way of pushing it forward into a skilled art. Like us, the untrained pharmacists would rub a dock over a nettle sting or eat some fennel to relieve bloating, but the Romans were the front runners in the new-found science of chemistry, which they eventually shared with us in the UK after the hundred years or so of occupation. I'm not wishing to be ungrateful to the Romans, as they gave us so much in the way of new forms of medicine, housing and the best way to grow grapes, amongst other things (reminds me of a scene from the *Life of Brian*). Just wish they'd stuck around a bit longer so that we could have made life a bit better for us all. Their hasty retreat from Britain to fight the invading Saracens and Moors of the Middle East left us in a right pickle. Their empire's downfall was a combination of over-expansion and in-house fighting plus the up and coming force of religious conflict.

The plants brought in from far afield represented a mini invasion amongst the native plants, although it was a good thing for the general health of the inhabitants of Britain. Already established by the Romans were the bay and sweet chestnut – all too familiar in today's landscape – both related to our native hillside family, but yet to be fully introduced. The Mediterranean groups had a sweeter appeal to the Romans for culinary and construction purposes, and they adjusted well to the British climate, with acceptance by the locals. The humble pea and carrot were also brought to the table for the first time, shared by the growers of the Middle East, so the vetch in the fields and meadows had its common ancestor turn up on its doorstep in the form of the pea. It was curious why humans hadn't yet cultivated the vetch for the benefit of the soil's structure, as this tough little legume would also serve to make other natives like wild barley become more disease resistant. However, the wild barley had a bit longer to wait until agriculture caught up. The local vetch tried as it might to have a meeting with its relative, the edible pea, on many occasions, but her patience would have to extend a little longer for such an introduction.

What was also good for the bees within Britain was the appearance of the apple and pear kindly brought over by the Romans. Our country lacked much sweet-tasting fruit, having mainly the wild cherry or the sloe of the blackthorn. The bramble was one that had a free spirit and rambled where it chose. The new fruits, along with vines, grew within the confines of a Roman villa or farmland; they initially seldom mixed with the local plants due to their neat planted rows created to maximise fruit production. The fruits were a product of control by the Romans, loved by the bees and also enjoyed by the nuisance wasp.

The young imported tree saplings made first contact with the meadow grasses when the grasses gave them a chance to establish their roots in the rich meadow pasture, and helped them understand and live with the cold frosts and cruel winters, when lock down was really important to all plants on the surface. Then once the trees were old enough to bear fruit, the grasses cushioned their offspring or windfalls on the ground for the collecting humans to carry away for a feast. The fruit trees like the apple were happy to provide a sweet fruit to share with all of those caring to enjoy. They remembered, though, the times when their seed was freely dispersed like the other plants in the wild, and for some reason they realised that one day many plants would experience a similar fate. Their early adjustment to their growers was to be something that they saw as giving a future to their seed – who knows, perhaps their evolution would produce more varieties and colours the world over. The bramble and blackthorn were less convinced of this happening to them as they had a dogged determination not to allow it – their thorny disposition gave them a reason to dislike any change. The gooseberry on the other hand was less sceptical than his angry cousins. He took every chance to invite humans to realise his potential within the pies, cakes and desserts of the woodland edge.

Quercus, Fraxinus and Corylus were still there, a little taller and a lot wider. It's amazing what middle age does to you, isn't it? Quercus had lost another large limb due to a lightning strike. He was over it but it took a long time for him to realise his own weakness within the universe. He was strong enough to shoulder the burden of the strike, though, and was only too pleased that he took the hit rather than his weaker friends. This moment of the planet's rage had a 100-1 chance of hitting him, and he realised this and took it on the chin. It also made him wiser, while his midriff got wider below him. One good thing was that Corylus had grown well amongst the two giants of Fraxinus and Quercus, spindly as she was, and as the humans were no longer coppicing her, her branches were able to spread naturally – not quite reaching the dizzy heights of the taller trees but holding her own amongst her friends. Well it added a fresh conversation point in the late summer evenings, her saying things like, 'I thought I had it in me but was so uncertain I could achieve it.' Her humble self-congratulation was welcomed by Quercus and Fraxinus, and as it pleased them to see her happy they weren't going to piss on her fire.

Dark Ages / Middle Ages

The meadow was the only really managed site amongst the plants, as the humans from afar saw the potential grazing benefits for their new breeds of cattle, sheep and domesticated pigs, all from the spoils of the retreating Roman legions. The invaders left in such a hurry they forgot to take their belongings with them; the tribes though, a little more civilised by Roman rule, had become a bit cleverer. Trained in skills of carpentry and building, plus new agricultural skills, they began to get on with things and survived the unexpected break up of normal daily life and rule. The odd hoard of gold might have been found, any horses discarded by the legions were able to run free again, and the locals had first dibs on anything else left behind. The 'dark ages' were upon us, and a state of limbo existed amongst the people of the country until a new breed of invader took control. Strangely enough, though, the landscape around them had also changed slightly – the moor was less boggy due to the elevation of road and path, the river was less wide due to the newly irrigated streams, and what once was heathland and moor was a thicker cover of woodland. All these changes were to the benefit of humans; the plants and trees as always just went with the flow. It wasn't too long before normal service was resumed. The plants left by the Romans had settled in well, but crops like wheat and barley again took prevalence over most varieties, which benefited only a handful of insects and mammals. The meadows left fallow were homes to ten times that, purely because the marching legions were gone so the food production was less needed on the open plains and hillsides. The result was a watered down essence of what had once been there in the form of smallholdings and outbuildings. Local warlords would take charge in a post Romano-British country if only to protect themselves against the threat of the very frequent Saxon raids on the east coast. Tribes from Scotland invaded the north, combined with the Irish raids to the west. Must have been a truly mad place to live in, not knowing who was going to turn up next.

The Anglo-Saxons had to fend off the Picts and the Scottish to settle the unstable throne of England. The plants and trees thought, 'Here we go again, is there no rest or peace amongst humankind? Let's just see how this lot gets on with things, shall we?', as they jokingly accepted the new arrivals into their fields. Quercus saw them as a less organised and polished army than the Romans; with their large axes and bearskins they resembled a unit of camouflaged mammals with bad breath. Fraxinus was more concerned about their large axes than their scruffy attire. He had already witnessed his cousins being felled downstream in quick short, sharp chops to create temporary rafts and houses, so he thought best keep his crown down and hope for the best. As the Saxons surveyed their lands from the valleys and hills, the remnants of the ancient hillside were visible due to the constant grazing of the meadows. They, like the previous tribes, saw this as an excellent vantage point on which to build a new hill fort. Most of the old ramparts of stone were still available around the hill, covered in a mat of fescue, buttercup and sorrel with the odd ash sapling for good measure. They decided to utilise this resource to create a sturdier wall of mortar and wood. A technology of stone walling and bricklaying was a skill inherited from the Romans, which made way for a new crude form of castle compound. The funny thing was that they decided to put the gatehouse in the same place as the previous native tribe. When will they learn?!

From the moor, though, the hill fort was very commanding, perched on a heavy limestone face with the gatehouse hidden on the eastern side. The newly built mortared wall would only serve to bolster its strength on the horizon, and the wooden palisade would provide positions for archers to aim downhill, overseen by the commander in chief on the tower of wood. The grain pits and simple structures within the hill fort consisted of a great hall plus smaller barrack-like huts made of timber frame daub and thatch, not too far away from the previous tribe's construction but built more strongly to withstand more abuse from the elements.

Gone were the palaces and temples of the Roman Empire, along with their fine wine and rich food. These were replaced by a more earthy food of bread, meat, vegetables and mead, although most of the poorer population had meagre amounts of meat and were mainly vegetarians. This was due to the hierarchy of wealthy landlords with only a few allocated the luxury of animals being prepared and slaughtered. The Anglo-Saxons were sociable eaters around a fire pit, and they were good at recycling every part of the crop or meat for things like animal fat for oil lamps (shame no bread and dripping then) plus hides for clothing. They were also keen fishermen, angling on all the local streams and seas. So there you have a healthy bunch of invaders that had a very scruffy primitive persona. It just goes to prove that people aren't always what they seem from first impressions, well at least until they're angry and bearing down on you with a battle axe.

So as the fields were replaced by lanky legumes, edible parsnips and dubious carrot, the meadow turf would be tossed to one side to create a new bed for these delectable delights to adorn any hairy Saxon's plate (male or female may I add). The grasses were used to this abandonment and said things like, 'Is that your worst? Come on, bring it on, it's only a flesh wound.' The newly planted crops would initially seem quite smug and superior, but they had a certain amount of envy and empathy with their distant cousins, as they were dealt the same contempt if they failed to perform well within the inferior soil type which they were not used to. They could only dream of being free from the shackles of their oppressors, and free amongst the meadow folk.

The Anglo-Saxons also fully believed in the healing powers of plants, nine of which were commonly used. They too were superstitious like the Romans before them, and they believed that sickness was carried on the wind in the form of poisons. I suppose they had a point when you consider airborne bacteria. The plants would both agree and disagree as their seed is carried on the wind – still, the humans knew best? Mugwort, plantain and stinging nettle were part of the collective group of saviours from the nine compounded charms who got rock star status amongst the tribes of the Anglo-Saxons. Combine that with the teachings of the Romans and you can get totally confused, but rest assured you probably got high on trying a potent mix of all of them – or worse, a dose of the trots. It kept the Saxons happy anyway, and helped them to a very old age of 50 or so as their life expectancy got progressively longer the more they experimented with the workings of the plant world. This trial and error was the makings of early medicine and cures of minor ailments all around the planet; so was the increase in Anglo-Saxon beer-making that certainly eased the pain for a short while.

PART 3
NORMANS TO VICTORIANS

Norman invasion

Iron and horse were king of most of the known world, and if you had the luxury of both along with plenty of them, you would be a king in the making. Wealth and following gave you the right to rule over your lower loyal subjects, and although thugs and thieves also came into this same wealthy bracket, over time they reformed themselves and became better, more educated people and more entitled to claim the right to all they had plundered in the past. The British tribes were built on all of the above, only to be replaced time and again by a bigger thug who would take great pleasure in kicking you off your pedestal.

The Normans were a bunch of French persons who claimed they had the rightful heir to the throne over a disorganised British tribe, so what did they do? Well invaded of course. When the Anglo-Saxon king Edward passed on in the eleventh century, the Normans claimed that he had promised the English lands to his cousin William in France, but the Anglo-Saxons decided to make Harold, Earl of Wessex, their king. Circumstance meant that Harold would be fending off an attack by the Vikings in the north, so William landed in the south unopposed. Well Harold caught wind of this and split his army in two to confront William at the little-known place of Hastings. The troops must have been truly knackered after fighting the Vikings in the north only to be told to head down south to confront Frenchy. Naturally William kicked Harold's ass and claimed the throne. Like all invading armies, they brought along their technologies and recipes of delight, plus reinstated a better bottle of plonk – all this from the learnings of the Roman Empire with a twist of garlic chucked in. Religion was also doing well amongst humankind in most European countries – Christianity was well and truly embedded in society after 400 AD. The apostles of the word had been turned into godly saints, only to be replaced by the priests and new order of monks and nuns, whose duty was to spread the word throughout all of the known world.

The monks of the time lived a solitary life within the confines of, well, a monastery, normally tucked away from the villages and towns to avoid any temptations from the villagers' evil tendencies. When the Normans built their castles and moats within Britain they also encouraged the monks to go forth and, well, grow and pray. This order of mild and meek men would be only too pleased to do so, as their vision of Eden was seen through plants and vegetables all around them. They would be the first real gardeners of the planet where horticulture and agriculture would be met halfway. They had walled gardens that were formally planted in squares or rectangles and filled with all manner of veg and herbs, all grown from seed within their grounds, and yes, they were the first garden designers. The lucky plants that had the pleasure of being cultivated had not seen anything like it since the Romans left, and, all neatly grown within the ideal safety of the humble potting shed or glazed window, they really felt special. They were also grown to help others like the weak and poor with minor ailments like a fever or the two bob bits. This interaction with man gave the plants a real sense of belonging within their community. The surrounding areas of the monastery were laid out to arable and dairy farming in a crop formation pattern not seen before in this country. It was widely used in southern Europe but hey, Britain is always the last to catch up with such trends. The monks would try to understand the workings of the plants along with their needs and preferences, and they were the first to embrace all the new methods to maximise their crop within a small space. As humans worked the land they had a habit of leaving areas to rack and ruin due to open space being plentiful. They had no confinement or borders so the cattle did their chewing, pulling and stomping of grass quite happily, and as they moved on to pastures new they left a huge amount of waste plus divots for new wild seed to colonise. The following spring would yield a better pasture due to the richness of the nitrogen-based poo, and the abandoned seed heads lying on the ground would have a chance to germinate within fresh soil poached by the cattle. This would be repeated as the roaming farmer returned to graze his cattle again. The monks thought, 'Ahh, what if we collected the muck store and used it on our vegetables and herbs for next year? We can replicate nature by digging or ploughing it in', and bingo – great crops the following year.

The plants had worked this out years ago through their natural decomposition, helped only by a wandering herd of deer or yak. A plant's internal engine requires chlorophyll, which is boosted by nitrogen in the ground, the result being a stronger, healthier root on which is yielded a better, more fruitful crop. Manure is also relatively slow release within the soil, which benefits the plant in its early stages of growth. The plants didn't know their luck when placed into a nitrogen-rich piece of ground which had been neatly folded and turned, loosened and watered, but they could get used to that. The problem was, though, it was all a bit too selective for the bees and insects of the normal pollen-rich pastures, who found themselves either liking it or lumping it, which gave them cause to look elsewhere. Clever monks would then attract them into their herb gardens of lavender and sage, where a fanciful bunch of plants were waving them in like a seductive temptress. To add to all this the monks would also give the bees refuge within upturned dung-covered willow baskets. In these the bees found food and accommodation in one hit, so the clever bees snapped it up. Little did they know that their valuable honey was secretly being harvested under their bee-like noses. Not so clever bee then.

Everyone was a winner though in this forced symbiotic relationship of humankind, plants and the insects, all masterminded by the clever monks, who put it down to God's way until things went a bit pear-shaped. This control of all nature's spoils can have a detriment to the environment around them – when you control a plant or indeed insects they have a tendency to rebel or become very unhappy, purely because you have forced them somewhere at no personal choice to them. The plants may need a little better soil than what's put out to them, or they may need a less rich free-draining soil on which to thrive. Putting aside any pH needs, a plant grows best where its home is or where it chooses to settle in its nomadic lifestyle, so this puts failure into the mix when people are not fully understanding of their needs. The humans didn't mind – they just replanted and propagated new seeds into fresh ground when all was lost – but the imported vine would also become less productive when conditions were poor. Wheat from the continent had similar soil type and temperature requirements to the native crop, so when planted in an area prone to seasonal flood, all was lost. Our friend nitrogen is also required in large quantities. The plants didn't give us any instructions or a rule book to go by; only through trial and error did we work it out on their behalf. In humans, too much of one thing is bad for our health, and the same rule applies for plants: a happy medium of nutrients along with the perfect aspect and light levels can help them thrive. When we fall ill our colour changes and we go limp at the knees. Our plant cousins share similar traits when feeling a bit under the weather, but as they don't talk we must make our own diagnosis. Gardeners like the monks shared their experiences to give the future seedlings a chance to grow happily, serve us with substance then reproduce for the following year. This cycle of life for the plant was short just so that we could grow stronger and healthier to help others less fortunate, and the monks passed on this favour to the poor on the sabbath every week. Their skills and teachings would then be the building blocks for future generations of go it alone gardeners within Britain.

This new technique was being practised not so far away from our home on the hillside meadow and woodland. As we return, though, we find that the Anglo-Saxon tribe had already fled, not through battle but through improving the drainage of the levels so they could integrate the drained land into their farmsteads. The new wave of farming techniques led to division of lands from the ever rising select upper classes. During the Roman conquest, local warlords of the defeated natives of Britain had been given special privileges from the emperor of Rome, primarily though to keep the peasants from revolting or being revolting to one another. They were granted a short lead on which to go about their day to day business without any future disturbance from the legions, and a similar system was inherited by the Norman invaders who persuaded the descendants of probably the Romano-English/Anglo-Saxon rule to accept such favours of land and privileges.

They were also given funny new names like Lord and Lady Fontigue or Baron and Baroness Beauchamp, some with a double-barrelled name, others spoken with a slight lisp of tongue. These unelected landlords would sit in all the best castles in the best clothes, with the best horse and cart money could buy, some even with two horse-powered carriages.

Their status would command respect from the unfortunate villagers nearby, especially if their land was neighbouring the lord in question. Everyone knew their place and their place was to serve and pay taxes to the throne. Failure to comply with this would mean land reprocessed and stock taken away. You know where I'm going with this as the thought of Robin Hood springs to mind – most hardworking honest people would be taxed so highly that they had no option but to foreclose on their lands, only to have it thrown back in their faces and be told to work their land for free. The nobles would then choose to feed them when it best suited them.

This greedy exploitation of the poor and needy was well noticed by the plants and trees around them, especially when the poor farmers' crops failed due to bad weather, or their cattle died suddenly due to a polluted water course. The lords would simply put it down to God's way, pass the buck then continue to fill their selfish bellies and egos. They would have done well to listen to the veteran farmer when the food ran out and illness was knocking on their door.

The lands were only as fertile as far as the farmer fed them and turned them with the plough, so to lose your staff meant your profits would drop. The division of lands would also have its problems when the population grew larger, and when woodlands were cleared and meadows ripped up the land began to lose its ability to cope with flash flood and crop pollination, the result being poor crops that either never appeared or found the land too boggy to grow in well.

This was initially a slow process inherited from the workings of the Romans and Saxons due to the local demand – not good, though, for the workers who had to rip down and clear the land ready for a crop of wheat or fruit and cattle. Deforestation was in its infancy within Britain. Like the Brazilian rainforests in a later time we had plenty enough to go around, so what harm could come of stripping the land of all its treasures for the advancement of humankind? The cattle on the other hand would be restricted to the boundaries of land ownership, their roaming habits confined to a couple of acres of initially great pasture that would be selectively chewed and ripped, leaving the dock and the thistle to set seed and prosper within the once ancient meadow. It's not the plants' fault that the cows would disregard them, as they only chewed what was palatable to them – it was the lack of land given by the human that made matters worse. It was so easy for a herd of cattle to starve itself to death on the land that was supposed to provide so much food, and the rain and bad winters would only serve to add a field full of pain to the cattle.

The plants tried to help their friends through fast production within the spring and summer months, but they are only as good as their own seasonal cycle when it comes to helping the cattle and all the wildlife and insects within their care. Desperation was the talk of the meadows until either the cattle were slaughtered or the humans moved them on to pastures new to fatten up for a higher price at market. Sadly the flow of kindness was reduced after thousands of years of prosperity amongst beast and plant to a way of trinkets and coins for the well clothed and fat landlords of the realm.

As the humans sought more advancement in their technologies and population, their need for resources would choke the life blood not only within the ground, be it quarried stone for the castles and churches, or wood and food harvested from the woodlands and meadows. They began to exploit what was gifted to them at the beginning of time, and the need for coins and status overtook everything else. This led to the lesser humans becoming as spiteful and greedy as their rulers throughout a turbulent time of back-stabbing and in-house fighting amongst all the kingmakers within British lands.

No one could make their mind up whether they were guided by religion or guided by power. As the word of the Bible had so many contradictions, that led to the superiority of the bishops and priests never being questioned by the uneducated villagers and poor people. The priests were happy just as long as their fire was fully stoked and a constant full belly of meat and wine was available at the stroke of a hand.

Law of the land

History like all things has a habit of repeating itself. Let's make a slight hop forward to when the British people have had years of French seed watered down to truly British kings and queens. It was a time when all the rights of the people were still under the control of the sword even after the signing of Magna Carta, which included the charter of the royal forest. This was a law carried on since the Anglo-Saxon period where woodlands were defined by hunting rights amongst the nobles. This kept the villagers in check if they were feeling a bit partial to the odd bit of boar or deer, making hunting reserved only for the monarchy or by selective invitation. Hard to police, I know, due to the vastness of the woodland coverage still available between the twelfth and early thirteenth century.

Our hillside tree family witnessed these jovial hunts as the royals headed to their designated hunting lodges near the coastal areas, but they couldn't get their heads round why something that had been freely used by the hunters and gatherers of past times was now restricted to a limited few. The likes of Quercus had grown up with the deer and boar, and he'd seen them in their hundreds over vast plains of open meadow and woodlands in an almost prehistoric roam of grazing and snorting. They would rest under his shade and scratch an itch on his strong ruffled bark, only to be scared off by a roaming human looking for a fast kill amongst a large herd or pack. Quercus realised that the man's action was from a natural need to survive and feed his family, and at the same time that if he didn't hunt the herds would have no formal predator to cull them down. Thus the balance was kept in equal favour to all the inhabitants of the world.

Quercus, Fraxinus and Corylus tried to make sense of it all, but they also heard on the wind that the royal kill was seldom fully used by the hunters, and that the killing was for sport, not for necessity. Many a carcass was left rotting in the wood where the animal had fallen, and the trees realised that if this carried on in a non-sustainable way there would be no deer or boar left to hunt. The plants as well saw this blatant disregard as a warning sign to all that has been built on the continued fabric of life on planet Earth. Although they had previously only taken what they needed to survive, it appeared that the humans were beginning to ruin the building blocks of life itself. Their selfish actions also meant that their fellow starving kind couldn't even take the meat from the wood due to the law of the land telling them it was all wrong to do so. Still, at least the upside was that a family of foxes or crows would have a short-term feed through the actions of people. Being wild and inedible gave these animals of the wood a freedom of passage between the plants and humans. Saving grace was served when the deer or boar hunt moved away for a few months to another ancient wood within the country, leaving it all fair game to the poacher and desperate people, although snitches and do-gooders would reveal these goings on to the local lord. The poor fox, though, would in time also be chased in the name of sport just to satisfy a pack of greedy landowners' desire to hunt a defenceless animal, with the cry of 'Tally ho!'

Winners and losers

The meadow grasses had their own problems to deal with, due to their brief encounter with an unwelcome guest known to us as yellow rattle. The grasses fell victim to this semi-parasitic plant as it locked onto their food production and drained all of their goodness like a fictional vampire. The ryes and couch took on heavy damage, with the bents and fescues slowly reducing their yields by 50 per cent; this battle ground, though, was to the benefit of the other meadow plants of scabious, oxeye daisy and campion. Had the gutsy rye met its match in this small unassuming plant? Not really, as the rattle had its limitations like all plants, being susceptible to the given soil type and weather patterns of the planet. The meadow council of plants worked out a way of tolerating yellow in that they just had to out-compete this little fella. So just as soon as the ground went less fertile, to the benefit

53

of the tall meadow flowers but leaving no space for the grasses to thrive, so did the lifeblood of yellow's food source diminish. The meadow plants saw this connection as the key to their survival, and knew that their path was controlled, like the way of the dinosaurs, as the planet chooses. Yellow just kept the meadow inhabitants on their toes from time to time, but, like all things, over time you get to slowly adjust and learn from a bad experience and move on. If there is any form of reference to present day prejudices, the meadow plants have already read the book, seen the film and indeed endured it. They have adjusted and moved on. They know if just one seed is left to germinate and flourish, their whole process starts all over again: as the saying goes, one year's seed, seven years of weed. Sadly humans don't yet embrace this concept due to their own personal needs of greed and control.

There were now ever increasing wars between the tribes of Britain and Europe. It was probably a blessing though that the Norman monarchy of England, their French-ness slowly being watered down, sought revenge on their French cousins abroad. The mighty oak of the woodlands would serve to be the best weapon to the English fleet of ships, and another ancient, yet to be introduced into the hall of fame, is the tough yew or *Taxus baccata*. This fine example of British strength has had a long relationship with the tribes of Britain, and is highly regarded in folklore like the mighty oak. It was planted by monks as a symbol of long life or eternity, or, because of its toxicity to cattle and humans, as a sign of death. Either way the yew had all its branches covered for a recipe of long life, and early Christians would also substitute its branches for a palm in a Sunday worship. A bit of a loner in its native wood, purely as its toxic needle drop would choke the ground of any life beneath its feet, its evergreen presence would give colour and berry throughout the year, providing refuge to the insects within its trunk and nesting birds.

Its power and strength also provided the fighting humans with the mighty longbow, due to its flexible and strong structure. This new technology would make a projectile of many arrows over a greater distance to rain down misery on a fighting enemy. A Scottish king (Robert the Bruce) would embrace the same weapon to use against the unwanted English king (Edward II) in one of his castles. Other such battles would be game changers against foreign foes abroad like the battle of Agincourt; still it only took a hundred years to finally have a victor. The yew's potential and secrets were locked inside its trunk for many centuries to come before its healing powers were fully understood by humankind.

Stories of conflicts within the European countries told of great hardship to both the human population and the plant world. It was told that many years of conflict led to the stripping of the fields of all that provided substance, even down to the last blade of grass which was once plentiful on the plains of Europe. A travelling army without the back up of food supplies would naturally revert to a skill taught to them by their forefathers, where nettle and sorrel were eaten to provide valuable nutrients and vitamins to a weakened body. All manner of roaming wildlife would also be put into the pot of game to fix a short-term hunger. The result was total depletion of the countryside around them, and the irony of it all was that when a stalemate was forced from both sides, the kings and nobles would feast on the finest food brought in from far afield. You can totally understand why the peasants were revolting again. As the troops returned home after a lost cause victory, they all sat down and thought, 'What's it all about then, what did we achieve, what was really in it for us?'

These troops were of common stock – farmers, and labourers – but the glory of war enticed them in through the propaganda of the local lords; their false promises of a better land led them with a field of empty dreams. To question their anger was treated as treason against the law of the land, so people at this point became a little bit more cautious in their actions, plus a bit more savvy to the needs of their rulers. The damaged parties of any conflict only serve to fuel the next generation of fighters, and we tend to learn from our fathers, be it good or bad, inheriting a constant cycle of hatred and ignorance towards our fellow man. The plants, trees and animals of the world hold no grudges – they only wish to continue their seed amongst all the chaos. They all, though, believe that one day humankind will listen to them.

All the common people really wanted to do was cut out all the political bollocks of the land, work their fields and provide for their family's needs, in the hope that one day their voice would be heard amongst their captors.

New world

Eventually though, something had to give amongst the rich and poor. Although Magna Carta only really helped the English barons at the time, it was the beginning of democracy within our country. Elizabeth I formed a golden age of discovery both in military and world presence, along with the early colonisation of the Americas. The Spanish and French had also made a claim to the lands of the native 'Indians', as the explorers presumed they were; this new world thousands of miles away was untainted, as in the early days of the prehistoric humans of Europe. It was thought that humans colonised the Americas through a small passage known as Alaska from the mainland. They naturally headed south to get a bit of warmth away from the snow and ice. While humans were migrating north from Africa, the tribes of the Americas were heading south. They had warring tribes like we did but they never experienced any real invaders until the latter part of the sixteenth century. By this time the European machine was far more advanced than their bows and arrows. It's funny how these European invaders at first were treated as gods for their big wooden ships and shiny armour, but it wasn't too long before the local tribes realised that something wasn't right when the strangers brought disease and grief to their shores. What would happen, if humankind in the future was to travel to another distant star within the universe and do the same to an alien race, beggars belief.

The Americas, on the other hand, formed a vast continent, a little bulky at the top but petering out to a thin wedge at the bottom. The British contingent chose to colonise the north with the Spanish sticking a bit closer to the equator – home from home, then, but with no one fully making claim to any of it; they were just flying their flags to punch out their authority – well, at least until the locals had something to do with it. If the Romans had mastered the seas or indeed the sky Europeans would have met the tribes of the Americas a lot earlier. As in Northern Europe they would have brought along technology and ideals that would change a nation for centuries, but unfortunately they were victims of their own success. Later on, as European nations grew curious about their planet, they became explorers of far distant lands, all driven by stories of wealth and greed. The local tribes were just on the wrong end of exploration. They, like the Incas to the south, advanced slowly. Their pace matched the landscape and plants around them; they were great observers of their environment. Like the ancients of the Mediterranean they learnt the skills of herbal medicine, and by watching sick animals they realised what could do them good; they put faith in the common ancestors' remedies and used these on themselves. This was the native way, and many herbs of the Americas had similar attributes to their European counterparts.

The colonisation achieved by European tribes introduced a trade in new plants to meet the needs of the insatiable European conquerors; things like tea, wild rice and tobacco. I'm not going to blame the native Americans for all the problems that tobacco brought to the modern world. This plant admittedly has a bad press and, yes, the natives smoked it for pleasure, but it was smoked pure, without all the modern chemicals of today. Its cousins within the UK are the woodland nightshades (*solanaceae*) but these lack its stimulant properties. Other cousins of this herbaceous plant were basma tobacco in Greece, which was believed to be puffed between 5000 and 3000BC, so no, we can't blame the native Americans. The roaming buffalo would discard tobacco due to its poisonous attributes, as the dock and thistle in a meadow were discarded by oxen in Britain. The natives probably set light to it one day and realised, 'Heh, this is calming, we'll have a bit more of this'; like all things though it has an acquired taste not suited to all of us. We can blame the English explorers of the time who brought back plants and gold to the royal audiences – well, Sir Walter Raleigh to be correct. Although he went searching for gold he came back with tobacco and the mighty spud – I suspect, though, that the Spanish conquistadors like to claim that for themselves. You can imagine the scene though when he came back to England armed with a rolled piece of tobacco and a dirty spud – what did Queen Elizabeth really think? A scene from *Blackadder* springs to mind: left seeking gold, returned with a couple of plants; what a complete waste of time that was. It wasn't long before the first chip shop was open! Sorry, the frying came a lot later and was claimed by the French. The tobacco on the other hand led to the global exchange of trade to Europe, primarily as its growing best suited the warmer climes of the plains of America, so there was no real interaction with British plants.

The spud was the first yank on our shores to be cultivated and grown by British farmers. Providing we didn't have too much of a wet winter or spring the humble spud did well, and our cottage pie commanded a nice waxy one. This country was slow though to produce potatoes on a large scale, due to agriculture being accustomed to cattle and grain, and potatoes only really being farmed in small plots of land or gardens. The Spanish fed their armies on this stable crop, and the villagers in tow adopted the crop to sustain them through long periods of hunger. A switch from grain to potato from time to time can't all be bad especially when you combine the two in a chip butty, where the plants from both sides of the world are unified in a match made in heaven. The potato also had a long storage life within a dark larder, and so providing they didn't chit out or rot you were good for a few weeks. Mr potato just wanted to seek out light from its many eyes, but its actions were not wasted by the humans, as they saw a chance of forcing the crop from its dormancy in the winter to the early spring. Like all things new, the London crowd had first dibs on the imported treasure from abroad, even if it took a few months to get there from the Americas. It took just as long to be circulated around the south west unless promoted by the local lords as the next best thing, or what the fashion of the queen's pleasure was dictating.

A fag on a Sunday along with a beef Sunday roast laden with veg and potato would become a quintessential part of British culture, well at least to those who could afford it.

Draining of the levels

Back on our hilltop a change was beginning to happen on the lower plains where the moor met the rivers. There was now a more major network of ditches and streams, primarily for the use of agricultural drainage, plus the odd road to join up the ever expanding population. Gone were the tribes from the hilltop, as they chose to settle on the rich pastures of the improved soil that had been soaked in water and algae for centuries, and they robbed some of the choice rocks of the hillside to create dividing walls and houses. The Elizabethan era would herald a new form of architecture of half stone, half wooden-framed homes, all capped with a warm thatch. As land like the Somerset levels was drained the soil was highly peaty, ideal for growing reed, straw or sedge. Funny though, how the Romans had brought us tiled roofs but we still reverted back to an old traditional method to roof our homes. Probably down to the cost of production of tiles, which is even funnier as the cost of thatch would prove to be the most expensive for house maintenance in the future. The use of reed for thatching was a good thing for the plants and wildlife of the wetlands due to the constant thinning and cutting for this valuable roof resource. The reed was only too pleased to help keep the humans safe and warm, and in return the management helped them keep moist without any litter build up. If left un-managed the encroaching woodlands would eventually take root, with the loss of the reed. The birds of the wetlands would take full advantage of the reeds during the winter and spring for nesting prior to the reed clearance. They were happy because their chicks fledged and then returned the following year with fresh bedding. Let's hope for their sakes that thatching would continue to be used for many centuries to come ...

Quercus on the hillside was doing really well without any direct disturbance from either human or friends. He had taken on a more chunky paunch where limbs had been lost through natural occurrence, and the cambium and bark had given him a couple of eyes. They were a bit cockeyed and not level but vanity wasn't his bag anyway. However, if he'd had a monocle he would have looked slightly distinguished. Fraxinus would take the mickey out of him but Quercus was having none of it, saying things like 'You're just a soft free and easy gigolo,' referring to his free seeding and random nature amongst the wood. Fraxinus was the joker of the three trees. He would always take the mickey and josh with his cousins within the hillside. But his jokes sometimes backfired, and he was left with egg on his face. Corylus would say to him, 'If you can't handle it don't dish it out.' A moment of sulking would soon follow until all was forgotten, well at least until the next time. Fraxinus also liked a bit of a tree hug but felt it was best to distance himself and remain the joker as a form of purpose and difference within the wood.

Corylus on the other hand was busy interacting well on the wood wide web and taking on a new social appeal. She joined up with the likes of blackthorn and hawthorn for some stimulating conversation about fruit and nut production to the masses, supply and demand and how best to keep up with social trends and markets. All rather high tech in the wood world, I may add. Corylus was never offended by her cousins Quercus and Fraxinus. She was the pragmatic realist, the mediator and surrogate mum to them both. Like most women she just got on with things even when the bark chips were down, a real tough and flexible kinda gal. But she also had her limitations and tipping point. Fed up with the bickering from Quercus and Fraxinus, she chose for a short while to meet trees of her own size and nature. These trees got on really well from young saplings, and grew up to solidify a strong hedge fund of benefit to all the insects and wildlife, producing collectively a high yield of production and prosperity within a field of uncertain trends above and below them.

Corylus had many a long chat with the willow of the once fertile flood plains of the estuary. The willow was disappointed that his destiny was defined not by the universe but by humankind's hand, due to the exploitation and greed they showed by draining the land for one single crop or animal. He went on to explain how initially many of his cousins had been used by humans to create small homes and boats in an unselfish and sustainable way, purely because the local tribes only took what they really needed over a twelvemonth. This new type of human took more than it needed, only to either discard it or waste it on pleasures of status and improvement. Many of his cousins, due to their soft interior, fell very quickly to the axe without a chance to put their case. Willow knew that all his family absorbed extra moisture from the plains to help balance out a particularly wet winter or summer, and he knew that his limbs had helped the beavers of the past build their dams downstream. His real secret though he held to himself until the local people cared to find out about it. His ability to provide pain relief had nonetheless been realised by the native Americans, and my god they needed it at that moment.

By chance, willow met up with Corylus by the muddy cart-ridden road-side – the humans chose this route of trees due to its drier path towards the coastal ports. He said to Corylus, 'Look at us all in a row, meandering down the side of the river controlled by the sole purpose of convenience to the traders going to the market on a weekly basis.' He had to laugh though as he witnessed the bulging carts full of reed or corn pulled by a very small donkey being whipped by an even smaller human all trying to get up the hill towards Bristol. The human's greed meant that his struggle was all the more pleasing to willow as the wheels got stuck in the mud due to the man's ignorance of the path ahead and the weight of his stock. It wasn't too long though before the penny dropped and they went around the hillside for a much longer but less taxing route to all involved, only to come back down the hillside on their return in a drunken stupor, clasping a small purse of coins to give to the angry rolling-pinned missus back home. 'Still, he reaps what he sows in life,' willow said. 'I'm just going to try and enjoy my life whatever they all throw at me.'

Corylus saw great tolerance in willow, an attribute really not shared by humans. She just couldn't wait to get back and tell her friends on the hill-side about the humans' struggle in soggy ground, as this new gossip would keep them unified for a twelvemonth at least. En route back she was fol-lowed by a traveller of Eastern European descent and appearance with a rucksack and crook. 'Perhaps he is one of those migrant workers that was heard about from the Home Counties,' thought Corylus. The traveller was taking the less accessible route over the hill, following the natural way lines of many a tribe or traveller before him. His pace was slow, probably due to exhaustion or lack of food, but either way he seemed to soak up the atmosphere in a very Romany gypsy way – he seemed to observe the plants around him with great enthusiasm. Corylus was intrigued as the man went knee high through the meadow of buttercup and sorrel only to suddenly stop and chew on the leaf of sorrel in an enjoyable foraging way. Fescue was also pulled out of the ground to reveal her roots, then delicately eaten by this fella. A bit of wild mint left over by the Romans was a pleasant appetiser to a palate of simple substance, only to be pocketed in favour of the blackberries on the rambling high reaches of bramble. As he moved into the woodland the man quickly noticed a clump of fresh mushrooms next to some ground elder. Momentarily pausing to pick his best choice, naturally the mushrooms took first place.

Weary and tired he sought refuge under the shade of an equally intrigued Fraxinus, who was studying his every move. Fraxinus saw no blade or axe, no shield or helmet – just a man that was well travelled and wearing jute and ragged cloth. The fact that the traveller took time to observe his surroundings meant that the trees trusted him. They realised that his knowledge of plants was based on a life lived out in the field, no weaponry meant he came in peace, and his simple clothes made him a man of honesty and trust … Well, at least amongst the woodland folk anyway. As he rested he opened up his rucksack to reveal his meagre diet of bread and cheese, but he now had sorrel and mint along with a juicy mushroom to add to the sandwich of simple pleasures. Unbeknown to him, when he released his blanket that had been neatly rolled up, a collection of seeds were released onto the ground. His previous resting place had been under a similar tree some 50 miles away. He'd repeated his actions today but had unsuspectingly carried some seedy hitchhikers with him. That evening Fraxinus gave the traveller an ideal recline of 20 degrees against his not so perfect trunk, and the thick sheep's wool woven blanket provided the night's warmth. The man must have been knackered due to his loud snores and grunts throughout the night. Perhaps that's why he travelled alone then?

Fraxinus enjoyed his company all the same and decided to give him a gentle awakening just after dawn through a little ruffle of his leaves. It wasn't his fault the small broken branch fell and knocked the man on the head, abruptly waking him. Fraxinus couldn't help but chortle to himself as the man jumped up and rubbed his head frantically, his insecure and defensive mode also awakened as if being attacked by an enemy. Something similar happened to a gent sometime after this. The culprit was an apple tree releasing its fruit onto a scientist's head, and the outcome of this would change humankind's understanding of the world's inner workings. (The trees had worked out centuries ago that what goes up must come down.) Well it certainly got our traveller up quickly as he lifted his blanket and shook it to release more embedded seeds from a previous journey.

This action would serve to create a new colony of plants around Fraxinus's trunk, like the unsuspecting deer had done with the woodland family.

This natural dispersal of seed in a randomly shambolic way was the beginning of three other plants making a home amongst their ancient cousins. These where cyclamen, celandine and cowslip, and their new home under Fraxinus would suit him quite well. After a few seasons Fraxinus enjoyed their consecutive blooms, with cyclamen making a second show late in the summer, and the ants also enjoyed carrying the seeds to new locations outside Fraxinus's canopy. Quercus grew a teensy-weensy bit jealous of Fraxinus, especially as his floor had just the odd bit of grass or marauding elder. Fraxinus saw the slight envy and jokily wound Quercus up. Corylus again made them see sense through the fact that the traveller had chosen that spot to rest. If Quercus had been in the same position at that present point in time then the tables would have been turned, so let's just enjoy the fact that it happened. They both realised that this was all part of the game of chance and nature's way, and that in time given the ideal circumstances they could all enjoy the same floor from the change of the wind or the path of the ant. Good things come to those who wait; they all had the same chances and shared their good fortune equally amongst themselves. Combine this with the early allium, bluebell and anemone, and a shambolic tapestry had beautifully appeared from the interactions of the three cousins: humans, plants and insects.

Horticultural revolutions

The traveller had long gone but many more appeared as casual observers within the hillside. The villages around the once flooded moorland had taken on a more solid appearance of stone and road, and their smoking chimneys indicated the ever-increasing presence of the humans. The church on the moor was yet to have its spire finished and it looked unlikely that it would ever get done as tensions between the nobility and the villagers peaked to the point of an internal war between the same tribe of people. A new model army was being forged on the banks of the Thames, and a country of two armies, the royalists and the Roundheads, was about to change the rights of the common man and woman for good – well, at least until the winner was confirmed.

Royal extravagance and waste from the taxes of both rich and poor was the root of all this, but not since the signing of Magna Carta had we seen such unrest. Naturally though Cromwell kicked Charles I's backside and

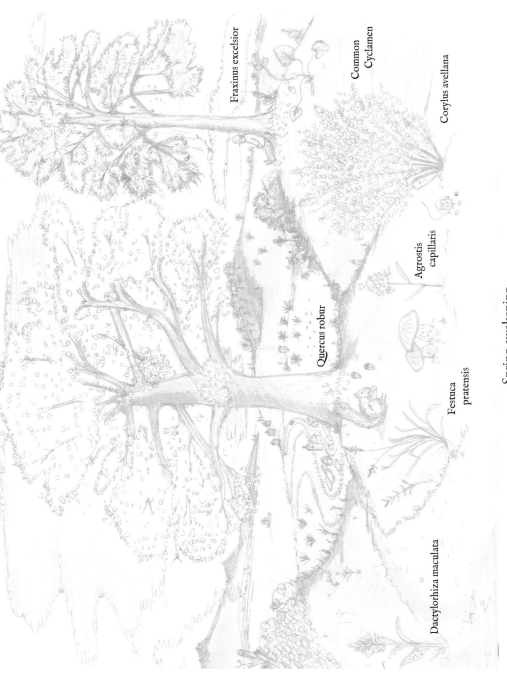

Fraxinus excelsior

Common
Cyclamen

Corylus avellana

Agrostis
capillaris

Quercus robur

Festuca
pratensis

Dactylorhiza maculata

Spring awakening

63

he was subsequently dethroned and executed, forcing his family to flee to France. After all the fighting for control of the governance of the country, the next real battle was fought through the people not being able to agree on the next step forward. This temporary government meant that the humans couldn't decide anything due to their egos and clashes of ideas (no bloody change there then!). The irony of it all was that they let the royals back in some years later to give the country a figurehead and purpose within the world. How bloody mad was that? Still, one positive was that Charles II brought over a bit of culture from France during his time of exile, albeit an expensive culture in terms of the taxes on the people, I bet.

The French people were a very flamboyant lot. They had come a long way since the departure of the Romans, without the need to expand other than the odd invasion of Britain, colonisation of the Americas, and perhaps North Africa? They concentrated on a unique culture based around art and fashion along with the cooking of snails and frogs … yuk! The kings of the country, normally named Louis or similar, would take great pleasure in over-taxing their subjects to fulfil their insatiable appetite for culture. Like the decadent Tudors, the French embraced garden design on a very large scale. A large part of their lavish stately mansions was surrounded by geometric blocks, and the shaping of yew or box was an example of humans' control over plants on a very large scale. Henry VIII had had a similar garden created in his home at Hampton Court in the far out wilds to the south west of London, as his pleasure was to hunt deer and entertain courtiers. Like the palace of Versailles in Paris it also had the creation of large canals and water features to stamp authority over all creation, but all this perfection took some painstaking clipping and pruning by teams of gardeners all committed to one overall finish of Eden itself. The kings and queens of the planet had all the wealth and power to fulfil their dreams and aspirations, and they, like their tribal warrior forefathers, just wanted to be history makers under the same sun.

All this neatness would be the start of horticulture within humankind's elite class, although I suspect the poor had a go at it now and again. The fact is that plants were first introduced to the humans who were less fortunate out in the field of life. When humans moved from being hunter gatherers to farmers of cattle and wheat they also had a loose symbiotic relationship with their environment, but the posher world of gardening or even the dizzy heights of design and horticulture always relied on the knowledge of the commoners. Their life skills would tell others of the needs of a plant:

where to plant it and what to do with it. Andre Le Notre was lucky enough to be part of that scene, guided by his minions of head gardeners at the palace of Versailles. The credit due to them was filtered down from the top to a watered down nod of appreciation. The other unsung heroes of these lavish gardens and palaces popping up all over the world were the growers and nurserymen, because as the demand grew for more ornateness, so did the need for a good stock of plants.

Tell me if I'm wrong, but a plant should live its life within the ground it is naturally sown in, with its perfect soil and aspect. To force a plant to live in a clay pot for the first five years of its life takes great dedication and control. Gardeners learnt the ways of the plants in order to provide them with their needs, such as nitrogen gained from the leaf drop in the winter, potassium from the burning of wood, plus the most natural source on the planet – hydrogen and oxygen, AKA water. These three elements served all plants well out in the field, but to replicate them took a bit more time and effort, especially when the plants are forced to grow in the confines of a pot, neatly rowed together in a field of control. The plants didn't mind this though, just as long as they were given the right balance of food and moisture to survive within the soil. It only seemed sadly unnatural that their needs were supplied from humankind in a totally reliant way. When humans forgot to feed them, they wilted to create deficiencies within their growth. They tried to tell the nurseryman that they were struggling and stifled but some of these men really didn't care as there were plenty of plants to go round. Humans had the will to give them life or take it away, which led to much hardship in that field when so much enthusiasm was given by the plant in its early stages of life. The lucky healthy ones were picked to go on to bigger things within a stately home or private park, fed organic matter in a soil of laboured double dig by the humans, and released from the shackles of their pots straight into a garden full of familiar friends. The clipping and pruning would then commence on an annual basis just so they couldn't get above themselves and bolt into a naturally small tree. Their chance of this would only be granted through the fortunes of their human captors. If the nurserymen failed to produce enough coin their nursery would be the first to suffer, which in the plants' opinion was neither good nor bad as they were just allowed to do what came naturally and grow. This financial hardship of the humans would replace the balance within the garden as with our friends on the hilltop in a randomly shambolic way.

One particular yew was destined to end up on the hilltop in a future time. Taxus had been cultivated from seed in a nursery within the home counties, but her story was of random abandonment by the owners. Her position in the nursery was at the back amongst the decaying and dying few, but she sat happily under the canopy of a field maple. The maple's shedding of leaf would be light around the base of Taxus, along with his fellow hedgerow family of elder and cornus. Taxus quite happily collected all leaf litter within her pot plus took advantage of the leaf mould compost around her base. Her root network had swirled almost to the point of exhaustion some seasons back, so she had no choice but to naturally head into the ground by carefully directing her tap root into the base of the pot's drainage hole which was strategically placed right smack bang in the middle – one good thing about human engineering of pots at this moment in time. Well, when this happened Taxus had no need to be supported by the humans as she had found her own way back to planet Earth's nutrients, her evergreen solar harvesters soon replenished to a healthy shade of green on which she just headed skyward. Then once the natural process of her production was tipped in her favour, the needle drop improved her pH. Sadly, though, the fighting teams of plants around her had no such luck and died where they stood.

The humans, who were totally unaware of this happening due to priorities elsewhere, were stealthily fooled as Taxus grew in tandem with her friends maple and cornus. If the humans had only checked the layers of leaf mould and ivy they would see that Taxus was still in her pot until one frosty winter when her pot was breached and cracked. And as humans have a habit of being driven by neatness they finally noticed her break for freedom, and her escape was foiled. Damn those humans! Or was it not so bad? Taxus had given the nursery a reason to save her due to her healthy leaf and growth so what they did was give her a bigger pot to live in, so the cycle just continued until the next escape plan was thought through. The humans also saw the benefits of her growing medium under the trees, so perhaps this was the start of the compost industry, or did somebody else think of it before Taxus? Remember this when you're buying your next bag of John Innes at the local garden centre.

Back home, away from this journey of choking wealth amongst the selfish and needy, was the hilltop crew, far from all the madness of the cities. They had experienced a little bit of the travelling armies of the Roundheads within their wood, when the soldiers rested under the canopy of trees. Their journey was heading towards the Midlands on the back of a bruising battle in Somerset which left them wounded and battered but keen to finish this war once and for all. Their defeat of the royalists would send shock waves through Europe. The French aristocracy would have to start looking over their shoulder as a peasant revolt is afoot methinks.

Viva la Revolution!

Fields of conflict

The local villages, huddled in rows along the dusty roads and footpaths, had neat stone walls and hedges to define their boundaries. The noble stallions and fillies were given the best pasture money could buy, the cows and sheep were second, closely followed in third by the pigs and chickens. The trees and plants on the other hand were holding back in the wings until a time of rebellion or war changed the percentages in their favour. Quercus and his friends, tucked neatly out of harm's way, would hear stories on the canopy telegraph about the battles their cousins had to endure. The fickle nature of the humans meant that they switched from arable to dairy to pleasure of horse from season to season – the reality was, though, that the humans were starting to become modern farmers and were planning their actions to serve the market trends. If dairy was more favourable over corn or wheat then they switched to accommodate it, and the nitrogen from the waste would serve to create a better pasture for the horses or a stag and his offspring. Just as the meadow grasses would invite their friends back into the field, along came the plough to churn it all up to plant wheat or barley. Saving grace came only within the confines of the hedgerows that divided the plots of land, but just as the trees within the hedgerows had a chance to set seed and join up with their woodland friends, all was lost to the grazing cattle's stomp and chew.

Fraxinus saw the plight of his cousins as they helplessly stretched out to touch one another and join in conversation, only to be cut down or even worse root-chopped by the savage plough. Some trees accepted their fate and adjusted accordingly, knowing that they would never be able to join up again – Quercus's cousins would stand lonely within many fields below him, giving shade and a good back scratch to the beasts below. Still, I suppose he had some company, at least for now. This was to be a familiar sight within the fields of Britain, where fate had dealt many trees a bad deal. If only they had been positioned on the hilltop amongst the limestone like Quercus then their story would have been so much better.

Well enough of this doom and gloom; it is what it is. Humans are just continuing to move forward in the race of life, the plants as always are being patiently confident about the future. The charts and facts of it all show that there had been an ever-increasing depletion of woodlands and natural meadows by the turn of the seventeenth century, with the cutting down of most hardwoods in the woodlands to create large fleets of ships plus homes for humankind within Britain. The only sacred woods were those in the hunting grounds reserved for nobility, like the New Forest in Hampshire, which had a chequered history under the Norman kings. Now get this: they had actually seen the potential of the woodlands for their hunts and by the twelfth century the peasants and villagers had all been evicted to make room for more trees – a victory for the trees and plants but a turn for the worse for the humans. The whole thing backfired though, as the land was of poor soil and was of no use to either man or beast. What a complete waste of time that was then. Although Henry VIII had had the sense the replant the oaks that he felled for shipbuilding, the same didn't apply in the seventeenth century. The New Forest was taken on by the Royal Navy for the local shipbuilding yards of Portsmouth and Southampton, but the planet had other plans when a great storm reduced the stock by 4000 oaks, so no one won. The sad story of the decimation of the woodlands within Britain, which were only protected by royal favour or site location, was by far the biggest damage that humans inflicted on the countryside.

Sorry, the doom and gloom surfaced again as I went off on a personal tangent about our environment. I promise you it gets a bit better as we hurtle through time in our own personal time machine.

Let's get home and relax, shall we?

Quercus, a spectacular example of what nature can produce, was humbled by the fact he was surrounded by such great friends, and through pain, hardship and the odd disagreement you truly meld a great friendship. Such grief and hassle had tested the inhabitants of the hillside – Corylus, a listener and mediator, next to Fraxinus, a blatant tart and bullshitter, had been forced to accept who they were and joke about their faults and differences. The view from the hillside down to the meadows and plains was broken by a thicket of bolted ash, all failed limbs and discarded branches. On a bright summer's day you could be in the deepest shade amongst the trees then look downhill and see the fields of the meadow families, all too pleasing to Quercus and co. They knew that their success had been built on growth and expansion but were really glad to see that the other plants were doing well. This would only be changed by the grace of the universe or humankind's hand, but the plants could all have a moment of contemplation to breathe it all in. Funny though, that the trees of the hillside missed the past tribes and occupants purely for their own pleasure of seeing how things were progressing. Quercus being very philosophical said to them all one night, 'To experience true love you must experience loss, and to cope with loss you must experience loneliness; it's what makes us who we are.' Fraxinus and Corylus enjoyed that sentiment and both sighed and smiled. Total respect, Quercus, you are truly a wise fella. Now let's get back to the business in hand, at the tree meeting.

At this point I'd like to explain that the trees of the hillside had a meeting whenever a topic of concern arose. On this occasion, Quercus started the proceedings by welcoming the family of woodpeckers to the meeting. They didn't bother with the meeting very often, so, as he knew their patience was limited, he took the opportunity to wish them the best. The midsummer bat displays had also given the hillside inhabitants much pleasure to watch – it seemed that the more obstacles in front of the bats, the better display each year of blind navigational skills to match any owl or hawk. Corylus agreed to allow more arching branches for next year's tunnel display. The expansion of the wood, though, took a little setback due to the activities of man clearing the north side slopes for more development, albeit only a small barn and outhouse, but all things must be recorded. Fraxinus worried though that despite his mass dispersal of seed in that direction, the cattle numbers were wiping out any progress. Corylus agreed to make her presence known there and advise the thistle and dock to move in when able to do so.

This led conveniently to Quercus's second point, in which he showed his understanding of the concern of all the wood about being surrounded by all that wants to chew and chop. Progress in expanding the tree cover was slowly being made on the east side, though, if only the human road didn't make a small line of division. 'More seed please, Fraxinus!' Fraxinus nodded and said he would deploy his family there late this summer. Corylus wanted it to be noted that ivy was having a hard time of it at the moment, along with the bramble, due to the introduction of a pine forest on the east side, whose fallen needles choked the ground. She feared that they had met their match when it came to any future growth within the wood. Quercus agreed to look into it, having had first-hand experience with ivy and bramble before.

The badgers and foxes, along with the rabbits, seemed to be doing well on the south bank of the wood. Sadly though the rabbits had to take the rough with the smooth, being part of a poor man's diet. Their speed would make them stronger in the long run, although Fraxinus did mention that the humans had invented a metal weapon that fires out lead projectiles to outstrip the speed of all of them. The fox on the other hand was slowly popping off the local chicken population down in the village, leading to a higher demand for hazel to keep the chicken runs free of predators. Corylus was just happy to oblige as it kept her in check, which gave more habitat for the field mouse, then subsequently a bit more light for either Fraxinus or the meadow flowers.

So ended the meeting of the hillside group, and they agreed to meet again in the spring to have a good old gloat about all their progress, and promised not to mention any failure.

Expansion of the empire

As laws were passed and coin changed hands, the wheels of so-called progress continued to turn, making the city of London a world force in finance and democracy. The people were still being heavily taxed to pay for the roads and palaces, and commodities from world trade were being imported into the great ports of the country, along with associated smuggling to try and beat paying the duty. The world off the back of wars had created many large seafaring vessels that cut the journey time to any compass point of the globe to a mere couple of weeks – well, if you add in the odd stay in a port or two. Making the world a slightly smaller place meant that there was a continued squeeze on the landscape, and by the late seventeenth to early eighteenth century the human population was beginning to outstrip the world's ability to produce enough food to meet the demand. The plants of the world were naturally pushed to provide more and more crops for the ever hungry population. It was a relief that the Americas were conquered and populated to meet the demands of the people.

Back home the Georgians were enjoying the pleasures of their conquests and trade throughout the world, each building his own castle of polished stone and wood, but hiding behind all this wealth was the dark tale of the slave trade. As the British Empire continued to expand around the world so did the British ignorance and sense of superiority. The fact that life had begun within the African continent all those thousands of years ago held no relevance within the white man's need for dominance – they would question their heritage whilst at the same time stamping their ancestors with the word 'savage'. Many tribes within Africa, like the tribes of the Americas, never needed to move away from their homes, as they were content with what they had. Like the plants around them they evolved slowly without any rush to get anywhere in particular. When their cousins turned up with musket and sword along with all their fine clothes and culture the native peoples were just curious with an underlying fear of what would happen next. The witch doctors of their tribes were not much different to our Druids and the healers of primitive tribes within Britain, but the British saw their unfamiliar way of life as just pure mumbo jumbo on a par with Satan himself.

Naturally the two cultures would always clash due to their differences, with the victor being – go on, you guessed it – the imperial British army. As we well know, over the centuries a defeated foe always gets a bad deal, with their rights stripped from them and their lands taken away, and slavery was as present then as it had been during the times of the Egyptians, Romans and Norman conquest. But you would think that through technology plus a greater understanding of the world the use of slavery would no longer be necessary. Wrong. The Georgian period saw one of the biggest forced migrations of African slaves around the globe, with the British tribe being one of the largest enforcers of this barbaric trade in humans. The large naval vessels and private fleets of cargo ships of the eighteenth century were predominantly filled with slaves being sent to the new world of the Americas and Caribbean islands in exchange for commodities of tobacco, cocoa and sugar. This trade would only serve to double the profits back home as the slaves either worked on the plantations for nothing or were sold to other traders for the price of a bag of cotton. The luckier Africans or indentured servants would be trained to work in the large houses of the wealthy traders around the country, labelled as their own property to do as the owner wished, until, elderly and broken, they were sold at market. I personally see the period of slavery as a step back in humankind's evolution – so much wrong done to the people who helped to forge the world we know today. But hey, that's apparently change for the better?

Stately homes and gardens

The result of all this was that Britain's wealthiest were able to build bigger and better stately homes in the countryside as a rural retreat from the busy coin-counting tables in London. Wanting to escape the smog and threat of disease served on the capital, they opted to extend their egos by pursuing a clean living life out in the sticks, where the air was clean and the labour was cheap; a place to be happily ignorant and switch orf ... They were able to commission architects and builders to create a home fit for a king or queen, just don't mention how much it cost. These builds would normally take 50-plus years due to their size and scale plus the extravagance of their brief. Along with all this splendour were the grounds that surrounded their homes. Front and centre stage, please, Lancelot 'Capability' Brown, an up and coming landscape architect in his field. His inspiration or hero was the great Andre le Notre of Versailles fame. This guy Brown had the opportunity to fulfil his ideals of gardens on a very large scale with an unlimited budget and no questions asked – 'Just give me something to make me look great amongst my friends and competitors.' I do admire his vision, but the realisation of such grand plans was to the detriment of the original ecology of the land he was engaged to master and tame. The local plants and trees were in for a big shock, I can tell you.

Mr Brown's concept and design was completely radical. Unlike his predecessors, who based their designs on long canals, geometric shapes, and driveways flanked with rows of trees leading up to the stately home, Brown wanted the estate to look 'natural', with curving lakes and rivers, hills and valleys. There were also large scale open spaces of lawn finely clipped by an army of hidden workers tucked away out of sight. Such perfection required a massive amount of clearing and digging, before mechanised armies of navvies would painstakingly dig and toil soil into carts. Blisters and aching limbs were part of the norm. Massive forest depletion was embarked upon to create the perfect view or scenery, along with the eviction of any poor tenant who lived within view of the house. (If they couldn't see it from their window it wasn't their problem.) Natural water courses were diverted to fill the artificial lakes to be stocked with tropical fish of koi and such like, then to cap it all the odd folly or structure was placed within the landscaped rolling slopes to give a simple splendid focal point. The grandchildren were the first to fully enjoy the fruits of grandpapa's money, all to be lost on the turn of a card or a sure bet.

The real damage was to be to the local area on a long lasting legacy, as the depletion of the woods would not only serve to reduce the habitat for all the millions of insects but also for the wildlife who lived within the woods. Storms would then create flooding in the lower villages due to the trees' absence (soil erosion) plus the diverted river courses that channelled the water to the seas. The result of this was that people were made homeless, plus a family of otters was left without any source of materials with which to build their homes. The economic knock on would affect the greedy landlord's staff, thus creating even more misery. To cap it all the lord at the top of the hill ate venison and drank fine wine and scoffed at all the grief around him. As the logs piled up in a timber yard, the wood was unceremoniously ditched down a steep bank to make room for more desecration of ancient woodlands. Just as long as he is alright it's pull the ladder up and sod the rest. What took thousands of years to mature took less than half a century to destroy, with similar stately homes popping up across the once safe rural landscape, where these actions were carried out with no real thought given to the consequences of the human's ideal of a 'perfect countryside'. Although the bloke was a genius, and highly regarded in today's history books, if the same things happened today people would be chaining themselves to the trees and diggers. The wild meadows struggled to compete with the constant scything of the ground, eventually yielding in submission to the dominant fescues and bents. The knock on was to affect the insects needed for the pollination of the neighbouring crops and apples, meaning lower future yields of wheat and apple, which squeezed the poor man's diet of bread and zider. Alright if you rely on steak and wine as your stable diet, isn't it?

Finally, all plants would eventually bow down to the control of the rich landowners. They did what came naturally and just moved away like a nomadic gypsy to find a place where they were wanted or at least undisturbed.

It wasn't too long though before a similar grand design was to begin on the slopes of our beloved hillside home – nowhere's safe and sacred I'm afraid. Up to this point the local villagers had enjoyed the slow pace of life, gone to church on Sunday and looked forward to the summer's harvest. Their homes of brick and slate now held little resemblance to the Tudor buildings of wood and thatch, as the manufacturing of bricks on an industrial scale made this bespoke material cheaper to use. No longer was the use of brick exclusive to the palaces like Hampton Court or a grand civic hall. A Georgian house or indeed farmhouse was simply built in a square box shape, with arched front door and symmetrical windows. Only the wealthy few would have a lot of windows due to the stupid window tax of the time, so to have more windows meant more status amongst your neighbours. This leads me back home where the villagers / landowners had become people of status due to their hard work, clever entrepreneurial decisions and their choice of farming trends, plus getting the right workforce to work for them at a good rate and providing them with substance and a roof over their heads. This age of the self-made man had turned a commoner into a landowner and a leader of men. Tribal loyalty was still present in a world of coin and 'what's in it for me?', but the harvest would bring the community together. Plants and humans would chew the cud over the year's highs and lows; relationships and friendships were forged over a ploughman's lunch washed down with the odd flagon of zider.

The annual harvest was a high point of the farming year, and a chance to have an unofficial meeting of landowners to air their differences plus to be collectively willing to talk through any sticky subjects. They would also proudly display their produce, which led to the friendly banter of competition. The plants enjoyed all the focus on them, especially when their master got the prize rosette for his corn or bag of spuds. Yokels would also congregate now and again at the many boozers that had popped up within the parish, some found there more often than others may I add – you know the type, red nose, ear of barley in the mouth, clay pipe etc. These dark and smoky public houses would be the offices for most of the commoners, where deals of simple trade were done, some illegal, others seemingly fair after a couple of pints. You could find the next day's work within the pub along with all the local gossip. Pub names like the Ring of Bells, the Butcher's Arms and the Plough were part of the local community, and the landlords, like the priest and the butcher, were popular people within village society. Local councils were made up of people who enjoyed such popularity.

It was at around this time that a travelling gentlemen passed by one fine English morn. He had time to briefly stop and stare at the beautiful scenery on the hillside. With notebook in hand and a head full of words of rhyme and rhythm, he chose to sit on a mossy mound overlooking the fields and cottages. Quercus was intrigued by his presence and asked his fellow trees to try and decipher what he was scribbling down. But no sooner had he arrived than he was on his way. With hands locked tight behind his back he promptly made haste down the hillside path. It was heard some time later that a certain poet called Samuel T Coleridge was known to frequent the area and had subsequently written many a fine verse about his travels. The hillside team were just proud to be part of it all, although I suspect not in word but in mind and spirit. They just provided the ideal moment of inspiration.

Box
Buxus sempervirens

female

male

Cherry Plum
Prunus cerasifera

Buddleia
Buddleia davidii

Taming the land: From informal to formal

Rural crafts

Life was hard but the rewards could be fruitful if you were clever and savvy with your coins. The farmers would also try to avoid any dealings with the local officials, preferring the relaxed black market with their colleagues from the local pub. This gave them time to enjoy what was put in front of them in a Pop Larkin lifestyle, giving them more time to care about their fields and stock. They understood the lie of the land, when not to allow the cattle to graze in the winter due to the rising flood water, plus the best field for good pasture in the summer. They managed their hedgerows in a neat and tidy way, keeping them stock-proof from the early spring lambing season, and they enjoyed the glut of berries in the late summer.

Corylus was pleased to be part of this, along with her fellow hedgerow trees like hawthorn and blackthorn – they liked being kept in check as it made them strong and productive. The introduction of hedge laying was the new thing in the eighteenth to nineteenth century, when boundaries were creating the patchwork quilt of fields all around Britain. If left unchecked the hedgerows would soon revert to tall trees which served no great purpose to the safekeeping of the farmers' stock. Corylus was happy to oblige to the slash and lay from the steel axe and billhook, but hawthorn along with blackthorn took some more gentle persuasion. The result though was a uniform tamed hedge that was cheaper to maintain than any dividing ditch or stone wall. Once laid, the hedgerow provided not only a network for wild animals to live and feed in, but also an ideal nesting place for small birds, all safely tucked up in a thorny fortress. Bramble and dog rose would then be free to wander nonchalantly through the branches to give the humans ideal pickings when the fruit was ripe. All this from the workings of a farmer who studied the ways of the plants around him. Although it was probably initially realised through a fit of anger when trying to chop his way through a gap in the field, his action would make him see the great inner strength of the likes of Corylus, providing you don't take away too much bark or root.

Once the hedge had fully matured and naturally headed upwards towards the sky the hedgerow plants of bluebell, wild garlic and anemone returned from their slumber, only to be replaced in the early summer by herb robert and celandine. This flow of plants from their woodland ancestry would have the chance to release their seeds on these networks of hedges, making them their own personal highway of growth towards other woodlands and fields. Communication was then possible between each ancient woodland as their path was not blocked, and when the humans let a field rest or go fallow the woodland plants then saw their chance to expand even further. If left unchecked they would make good progress until the plough's return in the course of crop rotation.

The cold temperatures of the winter sealed the open wounds of the recently laid hedge, and were a reminder to all plants and humans that the ice age cycle was still present within the planet's history. It's hard to think that through an icy thick covering of snow any plants would survive, but plants are hardy types; they enjoy the hard winters to dry out the land back to its crystalline form, locking in all the right nutrients for a spring splurge of growth. Humans on the other hand are less tolerant of the cruel winters. Nonetheless they have endured many winters since their time on the planet began. The winter just makes them work harder if they are to keep warm and survive. At first though, when humans first invented fire, they only burnt what was needed within their small caves or huts. However, the increase in population had started to put a slight strain on the woods' stocks, as the trees had already endured the loss of woodland due to agriculture and road. Could they keep up with the humans' demand for winter fuel? The fact that the local lords or landlords owned most of the woods could have served to slow down the felling of trees by the local contingent, but the truth is that the locals did their chopping in the night to avoid capture by the sheriffs.

At this point no one saw the advantage of planting more trees to sustain warmth for the future instead of the productive money-spinners of apple and pear. The answer to their grief was staring right at them, but they chose instead to be complacent, assuming that there was plenty to go around. Thankfully though, the winters peaked and troughed in their severity, which allowed a slight respite for the trees. The only thing going on in woodland development was the replanting of oak for the future battleships of the Royal Navy. This idea was inherited from Henry VIII, whose love of hunting and power gave the mighty oak a lasting legacy.

Quercus was proud to be part of that legacy but was worried for his friends or indeed his own fate when the last tree was left standing on the hillside, and humans had moved away from the safety of the hill fort to colonise the lower levels for an easy dig and flat land, all hugging the dusty roads that followed the water's edge. This would mean that the hillside was a spent force and served no purpose to the locals, plus the rise in cannon and gun meant that a castle or hill fort would be a sitting duck if it came under fire.

Industrial revolution

Quercus and co saw the threat of woodland depletion, over-grazing of meadows and the slackening and softening of the human happen all around them from the safety of their hilltop. They had witnessed both good and bad from their neighbours over time, it bothered them, though, that after all the fuss of worrying about the threat to their existence from the axe or saw, it all seemed to stop so abruptly. The humans' chimneys still continued to smoke day in day out, without any message of any forest reduction locally, and this made them think what's it all about then? Corylus sent out a message down the hedgerow highway to find out what was going on.

They were puzzled further still as they saw the humans' log piles still full from the previous season; what was present instead was a new box or bunker full of black rocks. Well after close examination of a piece that had been kicked into the hedge, the trees made a great discovery about the rock due to its chemical structure. It appeared to be the deposits of their ancient ancestors way back to the Jurassic period in a kind of fossilised form, and, like wood, once it was placed in a fire it provided a long lasting heat for the humans to enjoy. Corylus then thought, 'Hang on, this must have taken millions of years to form beneath the ground's surface.' The ferns of the wood also saw the resemblance of this black rock to their own genes, which was welcoming but on the other hand quite spooky.

Well this black rock known to humankind as coal was about to change the world we live in. The trees and plants had always noticed a continual increase in humankind's population due to their increasing carbon release, which was welcomed by the plants as it helped them breathe easily and grow stronger. This was why they were both contributing parties to the planet's evolution, along with the insects and animals alike. Like I said earlier, we are part of nature and nature is part of us, and it was inevitable that humans due to their technological advancement would eventually find a new fuel to use, coal being that new fuel. Who are we to judge the ways of nature or evolution? The plants and trees just followed suit so long as they were put into the equation. This new fuel from the remains of the Jurassic period would serve to increase the warming of the planet as it was another source of CO_2 to add to the equation of the planet's history. The trees and plants thrived on this new element given to them by the humans, plus it meant that they were relatively safe from future depletion thanks to this new super fuel.

This high burning heat source would also pave the way forward for the industrial revolution looming over the British people. All it took was a spark of invention, or in this case a lot of hot air, to produce the steam era. Mechanisation also played a great part in humankind's development, and combine this with the new super iron and steam and you get great machines that drive cotton looms, pump rooms and trains. The inventions by some really clever people meant that everything was getting to be less hard work and a lot faster. It fed a human hunger for years to come – no looking back, just keep going forward. All this also led the humans into fields of discovery in sciences like physics, chemistry and biology. The plants had naturally worked this out long before humans could stand on their own two feet, but were happy to just toe the line and not get too bolshy about it. Quercus, Fraxinus and Corylus enjoyed the increase in CO_2, lapping up the sun's rays and seeing their seed doing really well out in the fields of human abandonment.

Anyway, the Industrial Revolution gave us the railways, thanks to the early inventors like George Stephenson and his Rocket, all on a single gauge track of wood and gravel. Get me, sounding like a train spotter! This new form of locomotion would join up great cities like London and Bristol, all navigated in a neat, fairly straight line from A to B. Where it was impossible to go over hills they tunnelled through them, and when they met a river's meandering path they would build a bridge. The landscape of the countryside was being moulded by structures of great architectural presence, be it the vast viaducts of the north or the steel bridges of the Humber. As the train got larger so did its cargo of people and materials all under a trail of white smoke. The railway station would then link up the smaller towns within the country, and this would in turn bring additional commerce and trade, along with the increase in the local population wishing to stay close to the tracks. As the world started to get faster the world also got to be a smaller place, if indeed there is such a thing. And all this based on the plants of yesteryear who had lain in wait to be discovered and utilised again. Coal did have its downside though – within the already congested city of London the term 'Big Smoke' had to come from somewhere. The smog and polluted air would linger within the atmosphere of the large brick buildings to the point of blocking the sun's rays, while high up in the stratosphere the early stages of the greenhouse effect were being formed.

The horticulturists of London

Away from the smog of London lived a famous potter, Josiah Wedgwood, whose pots and cups were the pride of any Georgian home. His business formed in the potteries of Stoke on Trent, he like all entrepreneurs of his time built a business based on quality; he achieved perfection in production and perfection in sales and distribution – sorry, too many p's; that's left me a bit tongue-tied. Anyway, his wealth gave his son John Wedgwood the opportunity to pursue not only a career in pottery but also his interest in botany and horticulture (gardening to those who do it). He was also intrigued by the cultivation of tropical fruit and exotic plants within the comfort of his glasshouse back home, and like all up and coming botanists he had a lot of questions to ask the plants. Things like how do you grow, what conditions are best suited for you and how to make more of you. The plant's response was, 'Please give me space to grow within a habitat that suits my roots and leaf – in return I can supply you with an abundance of flowers, fruit and seed. Please don't stick me outside in the cold or in a growing medium that stifles my roots or waterlogs my stems, plus I need frost-free conditions for my seed to regrow. In other words, leave me be and take me back home.'

It wasn't all so bad though in the days when seven blokes formed the Horticultural Society of London above a book shop in Piccadilly. A group of like-minded fellas just wanted to share the skills of gardening and document it all on paper so all who cared about plants could learn. This made way for the lord to ask the butler what the head gardener was telling the gardeners of the estate to do on a day to day basis. The gardener was unable to write but truly knew the workings of a cabbage, which gave the head gardener with his limited instruction in English a headache. Consequently the butler helped him out because his master wanted the findings yesterday so that he could show off to his friends at the next soirée held in the 'grinds' of the manor house. This need for knowledge of all that God had provided to us was confusing to the plants when they went under the microscope and were dissected on that table above the London book shop; the gentry got some cracking hand-drawn pictures though. To confuse things even more for the gardeners, the plants were given names in Latin from the early plant masters, the Romans; sounded better though than just plain old buttercup or bluebell, and at least it made the plant names universal, as everyone on the planet knows Latin … don't they?

I'm not wishing to give these guys a hard time, as they opened up the world of plants to the uneducated masses, which gave the plants of the world a higher standing within society. It wasn't too long though before British society was sending plant explorers to the far reaches of the British Empire to study plants worldwide, bring back the odd one from the jungle and trial it in the field back home. The scientific advancements of the day also gave the preachers of horticulture ways to understand the plants' weaknesses and diseases, and to try to fix them then share the knowledge with others so that they could produce the finest blooms at their annual flower show staged in London. The plants didn't mind all the attention they were getting at the time, but it was really a lot of fuss just to please a crowd of non-believers in their true workings and needs. Perhaps over time they would get it? The thing was they knew they were not completely perfect and they had their fights with the fungi and insects of the world, but it's all part of the natural process – survival of the fittest and all. To take a lily from paradise and expect it to survive in polluted smog-ridden air surrounded by artificial light and inferior soil is asking a lot from that poor plant. They really did get fed up with all the expectation from the humans, only to be chucked out with the rubbish if they didn't make the mark. They didn't even get the chance to spread their seed or provide compost for the ground. What a waste. Others though soon followed in their droves to the shores of Britain in the name of research. Similar had happened in history by the Romans and the explorers who sailed to the Americas, albeit for consumption, not knowledge. It was when the English lords decided to plant them on their estates that they started the problem of invasive species, along with tougher insects and disease-ridden varieties. These plants' slow natural migration to the north had been accelerated by humankind for all the wrong reasons, but the humans really didn't see the harm they were doing. What harm could come to us after all?

Darwin

One bloke was really going to set the cat amongst the pigeons, and his name was Charles Darwin. Now he had the balls to ask and question everything about us and the evolution of the planet. This great visionary went against all known principles, especially religion and how we came about. The plants and trees started to clap quietly amongst themselves when lined up in neat rows on the nursery floor, saying things like he's getting it, he's our man, we have a saviour! Well probably not going that far.

Darwin's findings would shake the foundation of the institutions of his day like the churches and the hospitals, along with the nursery men and gardeners. To think that we all evolved from an ape in the jungles of Africa, and we are all common descendants of the fish in the sea – preposterous, they shouted, blasphemy, workings of the devil he is. Thankfully Darwin was a product of the greats within the Victorian era and held great stature amongst his peers, and this along with being born in the nineteenth century saved him from the hanging or the chop amongst the religious types of the Tudor periods and before. I just wish that his findings had been taken a lot more seriously and embraced by more people to help restore a better balance in the world.

Scientists like Darwin also saw a change in the world; they even had a slight inclination that global warming was starting to happen. They witnessed the amount of deforestation within the Americas to grow tobacco and coffee, how wheat production replaced the open prairies where once the buffalo had run free, and habitat loss on a massive scale. Like the British people, the Americans thought there was enough land to go around, so let's just take more and more each year, shall we?

This chain reaction, albeit very slight at first, would change the planet's landscape and delicate balance in favour of just one species. We are not the be-all and end-all of what's precious on the planet.

New builds on the hillside

Back home the fuss seemed irrelevant to the hillside clans of plants and trees. They were still stuck in past times where no one really interfered with their progress, and even if the climate was getting slightly warmer it gave them no cause for concern. This was until the humans started to build a large house on the west side of the hill, changing the slope by removing a huge amount of ancient meadow and trees. Quercus and co watched these workings intently, especially if the shovels continued to move towards them, as the humans, like many before them, tried to tame the landscape with stone and brick. Armies of men were brought in to move earth and rock from the site, but after all that effort more stone was then brought in to build the house. Due to the volume required, most of this was robbed from the hillside itself. This use of local resource saved the owner a huge amount of money by reducing the costs of haulage from the nearest quarry, and the new trend of housebuilding would only heighten the need for a more local supply of limestone within the area. The invention of explosives meant that humans could blast their way through the most dogged of hillsides; not since the early days of the hillside's history had the trees and plants experienced such a major land mass shift, the type that was created by the planet's growing pains. Gunpowder and explosives were the creation of man through advances in military supremacy over their enemies. As we learnt earlier, the bow was replaced by the longbow, which was made obsolete by the gun, and so forth. As the military found new technologies their weapons were passed down for the civvies to use as they pleased.

When the blasts started one damp Monday morning the whole hillside woke up to a changed world. The trees' roots took the first wave of impact, followed by their trunks and their branches displacing an early unseasonal leaf drop. Quercus, Fraxinus and Corylus were totally stunned and froze in suspended animation, but as the blasts continued they really felt scared and abandoned due to the quick exit of the birds and wildlife around them. The trees though, like all the plants, had no choice but to stay and ride it out, and reports came back later that day that the humans were creating great craters on the north side of the hillside. Most of the ancient hill fort and Roman temple were destroyed in the blink of an eye, making their presence a mere memory, and the awful sight of healthy trees that had been in their prime reduced to just a simple stump was unbearable for some to see. The axe and saw seemed to be the better option of the two evils facing trees. The insects hurried along the ground to find refuge, but what was pleasing to see was the attack on the humans by a squadron of wasps angry at losing their home to this massive explosion. But as the dust settled and the horse and cart moved in the site was less funny to see. What would now become of the hillside given that it was full of usable rock? To put things into perspective though, only a small amount of the hillside was blasted, to build and shape the houses within the area. The soil, roots and plant material around the blast site was just wasted. The hillside survived the needs of the great house, until others were eventually built within the locale. This would be a test for the hillside over the coming years, given that the humans' activity in the area was getting more and more lively, owing to the introduction of a railway station to the north of the village. This had primarily been built to connect the village to the local seaside town, when royal approval had been given by one of the Georges after his seasonal dip on the south coast. Well if he liked it, it meant that all should share such free pleasures as the bracing sea air and the invigorating shock to the nervous system, all helping to lower blood pressure and cure most modern day ailments …?

Suddenly everybody wanted to be near the seaside so the railways were built from the terminus of Bristol to accommodate such leisurely pursuits. To be near a railway meant that you were never too far away from the ever-expanding cities in Britain. This meant that the countryside got a bit more local for the townies to build a rural retreat in, albeit a scaled down version of the stately homes within the wilds of obscurity. The local farmers and villagers saw this change in use of the countryside as a bit of a puzzler due to the newcomers' desire to buy land without the need to farm and work it. The builders and shopkeepers were welcoming this mass migration with open arms, and with the local economy set to double in the coming years, the knock-on effect would be that the local children would have a source of extra income through work as gardeners and maids. The townies would also introduce their fashions and trends to the backwaters of society, making the locals slightly more enlightened about the world around them, just as long as they knew their place and didn't try to get ahead of themselves. Like the townhouses of Kensington and Chelsea, the gardens would also take on a new style of neatness, where meadow or field would be converted into knots, box hedging and columns festooned with roses.

One such new trend was our beloved Taxus, who was to become the focal point of the middle-class garden. She, unlike her deciduous cousins, was very slow growing but matured well in many pots over the years. She had travelled extensively in her long and esteemed lifespan and had gained humility and grace. A fine buxom specimen of a tree she was, with a fine root ball to boot. Her finely clipped branches and stems were regularly manicured into a neat topiary ball. From a bedraggled whip to a tree of distinction she grew. Quercus took to her well and referred to her presence as being like a fine soprano amongst a garden of tenors.

The trend for neatness and order was observed closely by the inhabitants of the hilltop. Quercus laughed as he saw the trees all regimentally lined up in rows along a track leading up to the large 'hice' or indeed house, concerned however that humans never really embraced the trees' needs well enough. Knowing that his growth and success was gifted to him by the natural selection of the planet, he had never been forced into a hole in early–mid growth within the confines of limited root length alongside his neighbour, and he had also never been supported by a dead tree stake in his early days until his independence was established through his own roots. His seed had germinated in the perfect soil and location that had best suited his growth for future years, rather than being plunged into a boggy puddle full of inferior soil provided by the humans. The gardeners did what they were told to do under the instructions of the boss. The London crew of gents would no doubt tell the boss if he had done it right when all was lost, and books on the subject would soon be available for all to read. Quercus enjoyed his space and grew happily within the sky allocated to him; he'd never rubbed his neighbour up the wrong way too soon in life. This good balance was also shared and agreed with Fraxinus and Corylus – their long friendship was due to their own space being granted.

Corylus, being the voice of reason, tried to see the good in what humans were attempting to do for their environment. Her non-judgemental comments both questioned humankind's intentions whilst praising their efforts, but she also acknowledged that it could so easily all go wrong if nothing was replaced to make up for what had been removed.

When the building stopped and the quarried land on the hillside had recovered from the random abandonment of the humans, the plants and trees that had been removed were only replaced by the thistle, bramble and nettle until such time as humans wanted more land to improve. This small victory for the wild plants meant the colonies of blue butterfly and bee were able to repopulate and thrive again. The plants' topsy turvy life dealt to them by human intervention would only serve to make them stronger and more determined to succeed. If the humans don't want the land, the plants will gratefully use it. Thank you very much. Ta!

Victorians

The village nearest to the hillside had undergone a massive population surge towards the mid–late nineteenth century due the economic benefits of growth and the railway. The expansion of the quarry was also a marker to all of the local success of humankind. As the large houses continued to hug the narrow streets, strawberries from a local village famous for its prehistoric caves brought added trade and commerce, so much so that they built an additional railway line to cater for such Roman imports. Close to the railway line was a newly built cattle market where all the surrounding farmers could haggle out a fair price on their prize sheep or cattle – the village was still very rural even if the technologies of the cities were banging on the door for them to change. Best keep away from the towns; they might want more taxes in return if we shout out too loud. A glimmer of hope was being introduced to the farmer's stock in the form of welfare for the animals under his care. Although it was mainly due to the need for higher prices for their meat or wool, the question was being asked of their owners whether the beasts were conscious or were totally aware of their circumstances. If the question was asked of their distant, wild cousins the answer would have been yes – humans had only served to knock them senseless through cross-breeding and taming them so that what they did was for the purpose of humankind's needs. So when they heard the bell they would waddle off to the shed to be milked, when they had their young they were not expected to keep them longer than six months, they would eat what was put in front of them, plus rely on humans to feed them in winter. Yes, they did have a mind of their own until we decided otherwise. The welfare of the cattle and other farm animals is our problem because we made it so.

When they are out in the fields, cattle's curiosity can get the better of them when they spot a group of badger cubs playing in the woods. Is it the badger's fault that the once healthy cow had been weakened by man, and that the badger had been blamed for man's own doings? Is it also fair to blame the deer for recklessly damaging a hedge, allowing the cattle to escape and roam free down the roads or in adjacent arable land so that they can seek fresh pasture and tasty crops? The way of the wild holds no restrictions to the inhabitants. Too right that humans should bear the burdens of their actions, if only to make them appreciate what is given to them by nature and the universe. It's up to the humans of the world to manage their business in a healthy and sustainable way.

Agriculture in the nineteenth century had its good points and its bad points. By the end of the century the number of dairy and beef cattle within Britain had doubled, and mechanisation had made the whole process of milking so much easier, although our local village still insisted on the traditional 'barrel to market on a wagon' way. Far across the pond in the Americas it was a completely different story. Going from invasion and colonialism to independence in a space of a few hundred years meant the now American people were a force to be reckoned with on the international market. Mass immigration in the nineteenth century gave the Americans a huge boost in terms of workforce and economic gain. The fire though was still burning amongst the native Americans towards their invaders; they witnessed the coming of the Europeans as a detriment to their lands. Buffalo were replaced by beef cattle, and prairie was replaced by corn or wheat on a massive scale. Their clean waterways were polluted by the industrial revolution, woodlands were cleared for new settlements and roads were built all in geometric blocks, save one Central Park to serve the need for a gentle stroll on a fine day. With their way of life slowly being stripped away from them, the native peoples retreated north to the relatively safe zones of modern-day Canada, only to be pushed back again by the French colonists.

All this advancement would only upset the planet's balance due to the amount of woodland depletion and natural habitat loss. The grazing cattle like ours on the hillside would strip the ground bare of all possible pollinating plants for the bees and butterflies, and their massive herds would also slowly start to affect the planet's atmosphere due to their waste, of which methane is an active contributor to increased CO_2 levels on the planet. It's not the cows' fault, but just like all things overdone by humans their actions at this point were unregulated and the planet's need to keep a steady temperature was not considered. Scientists from Europe observed this from afar, but they were laughed out of the class for questioning such notions as global warming and future drought. On our own local scale the methane levels were negligible due to the small size of our country and relatively low-density farming, but combine that with rising cattle numbers in other countries and you get a shared gas mix under our shared sky. Still, the trees and plants liked the warmth of the summers but craved the cold winters to control the insects and fungal airborne diseases.

The rise of the pathogens

Fungi have been the building blocks of life on Earth since our Big Bang coronation; they are the principal elements of LUCA. Fungi provide trees with valuable nutrients and water through their network of underground hyphae. In return, the fungi devour the sugars which are produced by the trees through our good friend photosynthesis. It's clever teamwork that requires an understanding of each other all in a relaxed symbiotic way. Perfect, don't you think?

Fungi are the true ancestors of all life on the planet, but we only see them when we pick the best of them in the woods. Our understanding of these plants is only gauged by whether they are edible or inedible – to look any further would be a waste of time, yeah?

Wrong. We have a lot to learn from these fun guys, just not at this present time in history. What we don't see doesn't worry us, but when airborne particles pass us by like pollen or dust they can make us sneeze or cough due to our own susceptibility. Trees and plants are just the same, suffering from airborne pathogens such as fungal spores, and as the planet gets warmer with less severe winters the bugs and diseases grow stronger year after year.

These clever groups of fungus can withstand long periods of drought and thrive on a damp mild winter. They are all around us and just need the perfect storm to breed.

The hillside was no exception to the behaviour of such fungi, and they were seen taking advantage of a dead tree or plant. Fungi cannot produce their own food so naturally rely on a decaying root to find their strength. Good fungus found its way into the diets of the humans through the yeast used in bread and yogurt. Quercus had noticed the spread of one particular fungus at the base of his trunk for some time, but he knew from the teachings of the ferns that it probably meant him no harm, so he ignored it. He put it down to his age plus lack of vigour to do anything more in terms of growth – in no way a spent force in the wood, just a tinge of grey like that seen on badgers and humans. Corylus complimented Quercus on it, saying that it added distinction and showed great maturity to have such an ancient cousin at his feet. Quercus thanked Corylus for her kind comment and went on to ask if Fraxinus was experiencing such a change. Naturally Fraxinus took it the wrong way and sulked for the rest of the day. Sadly though, other fungi were not as tame to all the plants of the planet.

A fungal blight which affected the potatoes and reduced the crop yields for the farmers in Ireland meant that the people starved and families faced ruin. Ireland, known as a pleasant green isle due to its warm Gulf Stream air providing just enough rain to sustain a constant crop, was the victim of unseasonal rainfall in 1845. This meant that the fungus spread rapidly and the spuds rotted in the fields where they lay. It's funny to think though, if the potato hadn't been introduced, what crop would have been used as a staple? Would a similar crop have suffered the same tragedy or would the fields just have been left to pasture for cattle etc? Obviously this was not the end of the spud on a global scale, it was just unfortunate timing for the Irish people. The fungi just took their chance to multiply while the humans suffered hardship due to the bloody damp weather. There's always something waiting in the wings to succeed.

Back to the glorious Victorian era within Britain, where massive improvements were being made in the fields of industry, medicine and imperial rule. They were stamping the ideas and culture they'd inherited from previous invaders all over the globe. The plant hunters of the world were bringing back more and more foreign species to adorn the great estates and town houses of London and beyond, and great glasshouses were constructed like the Crystal Palace to house the world's botanical beauties. Similar, smaller versions were plopped on the end of a Georgian wing for the rich to enjoy at their leisure. Some plants would make it in the fields or grand lawns of these impressive palaces, plants like the rhododendron and Japanese knotweed. Well they looked good in their native country – why, oh why can't we have them here as well? These plants' indulgence and need would eventually ruin much that the gardeners had built over the last hundred years. The plants, never tested in the field, would soon take over a native woodland or rose border like an invading alien species from Mars, sucking out the lifeblood of the ground they rooted in, leaving no space for our local plants to thrive.

A bad call, don't you think, by the Victorians? Still, they didn't mind, as it gave the gardeners something to do in the winter, along with other time-wasting tasks like double dig and leaf mould collection from the woods. Just keep them at it, Jeeves! These plants were never meant to travel thousands of miles within the period of their own life span. Evolution plus natural selection would have determined their fate; forcing them to a new location only upsets the ecological balance of the local natives, who were just not ready to accommodate them yet.

This period of time saw some great discoveries in the field of medicine, like the cures for common diseases like chicken pox and scurvy, and the discovery of penicillin, all by understanding the animals and plants around them – some admittedly by pure mistake, others by questioning why something happened. The mouldy cheese on the rich man's table would prevent his ulcer being a bigger problem, and the milkmaid working with the cattle made her immune system stronger against the dreaded pox. All these by chance or good judgement meant the plants had the upper hand with the humans' future – give them more time and they will start to understand. Botany and horticulture became the words for the understanding of plants, and the work of these scientists was catapulted into higher esteem due to royal approval. This meant that there was more money to be made from the plants of the world because someone said so. Nurseries of plants and the showing of plants had never been so needed, especially on the lawns of the Royal Hospital, Chelsea, where humans would try to outwit each other by introducing a different strain of plant by replicating their sexual goings on. Some plants, though, would be gened out by this, making them useless and sterile within their environment, but hey, they made a masterful display of colour all the same. Who knows, the growers thought, I may even have a plant named after me – ooh, that would be just splendid.

The bees knew that their actions changed some plants' colours and genetics. Humans only had the knowledge at this point to loosely understand the workings of a plant but they really just wanted to fuss and control. In the eyes of God we garden, they thought. So it's all ok then to manipulate now and again?

PART 4
THE TWENTIETH CENTURY

Internal combustion engine

The planet's storms were about to get a lot fiercer towards the end of the nineteenth century into the twentieth century, and as the chimneys smoked and choked the air a new machine was beginning to really change the world we live in. Since the introduction of steam, humankind had had an insatiable appetite to get somewhere quicker. The stagecoach and cart had had their day until the comfortable railways with cushioned carriages and sociable conversation were more pleasurable than a dusty, rickety, bouncy stage. To me the railways were indeed a brilliant idea that connected up large cities, towns and villages, all on a neat network of interlocking tracks, and the train replaced the barge to allow for more sociable pursuits on the water, like rowing and fishing. So from cart to dramway to railway we rolled on and on forward. Independence and freedom to roam and do what you please without any timetables at a speed of your own made the internal combustion engine a new force to reckon with. It's funny though how the car or automobile gave the same freedom as a horse but without the need to stable and fuss it. Beasts need taming; a manmade machine is mastered and polished.

At first the car was a very crude piece of machinery with all the attributes of a fine horse-drawn carriage but with a dirty great big smoking engine on the back of it. The preferred fuel for this machine was in fact the remnants of the Jurassic period in the form of oil or 'black gold', as it was known by the Texans. Oil wasn't a new thing on the planet; it dated back to Roman times and was used to burn lamps, and if you coat a big ball of hay with it, it also makes a great projectile when lobbed by a catapult. The medieval period saw the oil or tar used as a deterrent to an invading army outside the walls of a castle, through sending out shots of boiling hot tar. As the modern era dawned and science became a serious profitable career, everybody was in a big rush to prove their worth in the sea of inventors and professors. The focus was on this substance that burned well and had endless possibilities, so once petroleum was refined in the early twentieth century the pistons of progress really started to fire under the bonnet of all would-be automobile makers. The investors and mechanics were the first to put these horseless carriages on the road. After the odd crash, loss of limb, etc they perfected the perfect spring and tyre to cushion the impact of the rutted roads, also helped by the widespread increase in Tarmac, which made the roads more comfortable to drive on. All these new inventions were set to get the humans off the trains and onto the roads of freedom – independence and choice made the best way to travel. Little did the inventors realise just how much their engines would be doing to the planet and how the humans would come to rely on their cars in future years, and yes it was only a small explosion limited to the wealthy at first, but soon everyone on the planet would want to have a car on their driveway to show off to their neighbours. The American machine of skyscrapers and capitalism fuelled the beginnings of mass production of the model T, which led to similar models around the globe.

The next major invention, of flight, would also make a world-changing footprint on the planet's future. We had the industry to make the fast car, and the same principle was mastered in flight. Once the Wright brothers had managed to perfect their paper wings and propellers to create thrust skyward, had humans mastered the sky? Was gravity a thing of the past? The planet had other ideas for the contraptions created by man (eventually even the albatross has to land and refuel). Bubbles burst and balloons are full of hot air but humans still feel the need to get closer to the stars due to the astronomers' findings through their magnifying telescopes. They, like all scientists of their time, questioned the universe's purpose and indeed, are we alone in the stars?

So there we have it, modern times in their infancy, soon to be a teenager and quickly forced into an adult all within the space of ten years or so, and once humans had ditched the coal and relied on petrol the planet had no choice but to hold its breath. In an ideal world the scientists would have embraced the technology of the plant through their own machine of photosynthesis and perfected the solar panel. If hydrogen had been researched more during the steam age then the car would be far, far cleaner to run. Oil would be a constant, though, even if the propulsion was otherwise mastered, due to the use of lubricants on the inner cogs. Humans – still primitive – took the quickest route possible without any idea of the consequences of their actions in the long term.

All a bit jolly back home, though, as the local lord took possession of his first car and managed to ruffle a few feathers amongst the locals as he bombed down the lanes at breakneck speed, driving the milk churn carts that were en route to the local market off the road. There were no apologies as the milk was spilt due to being forced into the ditch, only 'Get out of my way, I'm late for a date with my friends at the clubhouse!' Three sheets to the wind with a lot of hot air to boot.

The hillside family of Quercus heard all the commotion as the horn was sounded and the abuse echoed through the valley, before the dust and smoke disappeared in the distance. Machines and mechanisation were still to make it to the village, save for the puff trail of the trains to and from the seaside, and it all seemed calm and less stressful from a distance, especially from the hilltop. The horse and plough were still used on the drained levels but there were deeper ditches and more of a camber on the road to counteract the daily tidal flood of the sea. Domestication of the wolf had given the humans a friend to rely on in the form of sheep dogs and Labradors, and Quercus had the pleasure of meeting them one day on the hilltop. Memories of his sapling years took him back to the wolf pack on the ancient meadows before there was any agriculture, and he reminisced over times gone by as the young cubs chased the faster hare, watched over by the wise parents. Quercus saw the wolf in the eyes of the collie, and his wolf-like stance and actions mimicked the hungry pack as he rounded up the worried sheep into pens or navigated them down the woodland path. Nipping and hustling them into line under the controlled bleeps of the shepherd's whistle and voice, the dog, unable to eat his prey, was no doubt rewarded with a good bone after a long hard day's work. Quercus witnessed the bond between the species as the dog sought a gentle stroke of the head from his master, but was slightly saddened to think that this was the future and the wolf pack would never return again. Still, probably better to have a memory than a lost thought or a grievance towards humankind, as many such wolf-like dogs would soon begin to appear on the hillside as they were leisurely walked to work off their idle fat. Some spoilt, others a bit manky; the eyes, though, all the same.

The local quarry had begun to expand even further eastward in the search for the perfect line of rock, and the industrialists of the quarry had at this point introduced more efficient machines to chop the stone up into smaller pieces. The lime kilns would burn and choke the atmosphere around the hillside; the builders nonetheless ignored the smell in their mission to perfect the best wall or bridge in the county. Other similar quarries in the area would soon be converted to produce concrete and Tarmac for the modern road and bridge on which the car and lorry would be king. Houses along the lower ridges of the hillside started to pop up as the quarry got larger, initially built by the local lords to accommodate their staff in rented abodes. These little cottages of brick and stone plus the much grander-style homes seen on the west side of the hill would utilise the rock around them or steal the stone from the derelict hill fort. Well before there were laws about planning, anybody who owned the land built on the land, no questions asked. No questions asked about the hillside, its history and the vast quantities of rock, and the fact that it was all held together by the roots and stems of a team of plants. Random abandonment meant that it was all fair pickings for the gable end of the house.

To be fair though, the person who chose to move to the outskirts of the village only saw the potential of the view and the proximity to the road; they probably wanted to escape from all the fuss in the cities like many before them. Time would hopefully make them truly understand the beauty that lay both above and beneath the ground, something that Quercus and co were willing to wait and share with them, as they were only too pleased to have some neighbours again. The humans had no particular preference for the surrounding landscape save for utilising a bit of firewood, with security provided by their thick walls and heavy doors. The introduction of water to each household was a true luxury to the homes around the woods, and with sewage issues covered as well, the ability to stay at home and not want for much left the humans isolated on their own terms. Their staff would provide them with food from the village, leaving them to organise book clubs and soirées for all the similar types within the locale. And when the cars, with the put-put of the engines, rolled up to their driveway, the trees stood and stared at such strange contraptions. It was such a good talking point though, especially when there was a newer, better model each year to show off. The increase in these new homes with a population surge of an extra 20 or so never really affected the overall shape of the hillside due to the select few that had the coin to splash on a new build towards the end of the nineteenth century. The simple folk and woodsmen would take it onto themselves to collect dead wood and kindling from the hillside, plus when opportunity struck due to a fallen tree they chipped away at it when needed. Coal was still the preferred fuel in the wealthier households as it required less fuss to store and use, but the poorer folk would nonetheless pick up the meagre scraps between each delivery. The use of coal would mean that the woods around the hilltop got thicker and thicker, and Fraxinus and his offspring, who given an inch would take a mile, were busy capitalising on this to the point of no control by either nature or beast. He would also teasingly set the odd seed at the feet of both Quercus and Corylus to just rub it in slightly, so a quiet word was needed by both to put him in his place. Corylus was always the voice of reason on such delicate subjects, and a meeting was called by all who felt compelled to listen and air their opinions.

Corylus started the proceedings by addressing the concerns of some new arrivals to the wood, like the yew and the pine who had recently settled in the northern wing of the hillside. They, like all the trees, were concerned that their stability of growth was both threatened and hampered by the encroaching quarry. Quercus tried to reassure them that the quarry would be spent within the next 50 years due to the bigger quarries being created on the Mendips and beyond, and so, due to the slowdown of this quarry's usage, it was highly unlikely that they would all become homeless. This gave the yew and the pine welcome reassurance after the destruction of the temple which they had held so dear. Corylus understood their feelings due to the stealing of the rocks from the ancient hill fort to build nearby human homes. Nothing is sacred, she went on to say.

Matters soon turned to Fraxinus, as everyone wanted some form of closure to an ever-increasing problem amongst the meadow families and wildlife, along with the other trees trying to make good ground. Quercus without tact jumped straight in and said, 'Fraxinus, what's it all about then? Are you going to slow down and give us all some breathing space or are you determined to ruin it for all of us?' At which point Corylus quickly jumped in before Fraxinus could speak, seeing that his crown was all raised and ruffled. 'It's not Fraxinus's fault that the increase in the gases in the air is making his sort grow faster, and it is also not his fault that the humans have chosen an ancient fuel to warm their homes. It is a blessing, don't you think though, Quercus, due to the massive depletion of the wood on the north side from the quarry, that Fraxinus's progress is great news for all of us, albeit on a rather over-indulgent scale …'

Fraxinus stood quietly and humbly nodded his branches towards Corylus, but Quercus was less charmed. He felt compelled to speak up for all the softer trees within the wood, given that his strength and character was held high in the opinions of all the other plants. Quercus wanted to voice the thoughts of the three absent at the meeting, those who were sleeping in the ground: bluebell, wild garlic and anemone. They had suffered the most over the years from poaching by the cattle hoof plus the massive loss of their cousins due to the quarry's expansion. On a ratio of bulb to tree the scale was 50 times the amount of the loss suffered by each type of tree or fern. This prompted the small voices from the outer wood to be represented by the grasses, buttercup and sorrel. They were so quiet they could hardly be heard amongst the thick wood covering, with sorrel slightly more muffled under fescue due to her lack of flower. Corylus quickly went to their aid and asked her hedgerow mates to ask them to speak up. Buttercup was their nominated voice as she still held flower in the late summer sun, and she went on to attack all of the woodland groups for their need to expand, and the loss of habitat for all when their family of plants was depleted down to almost nothing. 'If it wasn't for our friends in the hedgerows we would have gone centuries ago,' she said. 'We have not seen or heard of any orchids, any scabious or any vetch for years. Our friends have just disappeared from around us due to the expansion of the wood plus the workings of human-kind. We were once just as dominant as you on the hillside, we accepted your seed and moved to give you space to grow. We then hit a brick wall of roads and stream which penned us in. We naturally adjusted for a few hundred years, but then the onslaught of man's cattle ripped us down to nothing. You all talk of loss of land to expand onto; we on the other hand pick up the scraps everyone leaves behind.'

Well that put all the hillside in its place, as they'd all been so busy worry-ing about their own life without a slight glimmer of concern for the results of their actions around them. Quercus spoke quietly to all. 'Are we just as greedy as humankind, or are we just doing what comes naturally? I think on the next wind change we should consider the meadow folk – perhaps lean our branches away from them slightly to hopefully change the per-centage of sunlight on their patch, and if the wind is kind to us allow our leaf drop to fall on the north side to benefit the bulbs. Fraxinus, just keep doing what you do but spare a thought for the buttercup and her friends.' The meeting was closed on a very sombre note. Anger had turned to pity, which made the hillside a little humbler and wiser to their current position in time.

The ferns and algae on the west side of the wood just sat and talked amongst themselves very quietly. Their ancient path had made them wiser than all; they had seen all this before. They were the first to warn the trees and plants within their network about any threat towards them – this prim-itive jungle telegraph was unexplainable to humans but understood fully by the plants, time after time, species after species. 'They just need to be a bit more patient,' the ferns said. 'Time and the planet has a way of resetting itself when things all get a bit too much to bear.' This fingernail print on the planet's history is just a blink of an eye for the ferns. They are never in a hurry to go anywhere; they're just happy to sit on the earth's rock.

I wish the same could be said for the humans. The ants and bees always seemed to be in a hurry to harvest their food but they're really not on a par with humankind. At the turn of the twentieth century humankind was really busy building new roads of tar, with less rail for trains, and with more homes to build there was less land to rest. The UK was on a small scale compared to the newly named United States of America, with all that land of hope etc ready to be exploited by the human machine – so much so that in places like New York they chose to go upwards, outwards and underneath the ground. They were the world's trend setters when it came to technology and architecture; London would now be a mere second or third in the world when it came down to expansion. The funny thing was they left a small patch of land in the centre of New York for a park for all to forget that they were in a large city. The best of both worlds?

As the chemists and scientists also made huge advances in the search for cures for humankind's weaknesses it served to make people stronger and last longer. They had learnt over the centuries about the healing powers of plants but it wasn't until now that they had dispensed their findings in pill form. So as the willows sat on the river banks of the flood plains, their secrets were realised and harnessed to ease people's headaches in the form of aspirin, plus the antibiotics found in mouldy cheese helped cure a nagging infection within. All this as they filled their bellies with more yeast and sugar to help them deal with an infection and a hangover from excess, but surely there are other cures out there so they could enjoy their life into old age.

New methods of cultivation and trials tested the plants' limitations within the fields of the UK just so that we could bring the tropics to the cold northern hemisphere. I'm not wishing to criticise the horticulturists and their work, and I suppose the plants did end up in our gardens a lot faster than their own path would have eventually allowed them. Plus as Britain is an island, it would be a hard task for the seeds and roots of the plants to cross the Channel from the shores of Normandy, so the horticulturists just helped it all along a bit faster. The insects on the other hand chose to live with whatever plants were offered – as the pollen of plants was a universal food for them, who were they to complain? The plants just wished the humans would stop the wars so that everyone could get on and learn more about each other, but no, they must continue to blow things up and conquer. How many more wars will it take before there is nothing left to fight for?

First World War

The Europeans stood back and watched the USA expand, with a vested interest in its success. If they do well, so do we, they thought, especially amongst the financial world of Wall Street and beyond – it would take a major crash to stop them in their tracks. Anyway, Europe had its own problems to deal with, especially as their past wars only fuelled more hatred and prejudice against one another, prompting a Great War between European tribes. Humans' military advances only serving to kill more people on a larger field of conflict within the trenches of France, stalemate was achieved by the artillery and machine guns, with no one really making ground in a hurry. The invention of flight was utilised to drop bombs and rain down bullets to collective masses on the ground. The constant barrage of missiles left the fighting field a sorry state to see. Mud and splintered trees only slightly resembled a once wooded glen of meadow and stream. Hell on earth.

World War I was a global war involving many countries, and deemed the war to end all wars. Must have been the right wording to use after thousands of years of conflict – let's just see, shall we?

I don't want to go too deeply into all this as I really feel that wars just are not worth the bother. Humankind's natural cull could be achieved in a far easier way than by a bullet or a bomb. When the First World War ended the battlefields of the Somme rested and regrew with a blanket of red poppies, a fitting testament to all the bloodshed and despair caused on that land. Humans then adopted the poppy for remembrance so that they didn't forget the ones that had lost their lives for freedom. It's nice to see that a plant, especially the meadow poppy, would be a symbol of peace. The poppy on the other hand just took the chance to grow before the other plants took hold, as dispersal had already been achieved by the flying remnants of bombs and sodden trench foot boots.

Military advances were again achieved with the introduction of the steel tank, hand-held machine gun, oh and the hard hat – a waste of time that is when facing a determined bullet to your head. The need to kill from greater distances without the full guilt of eye contact meant that war got total. Generals in war rooms far away, playing out their games in the comfort of a warm bunker surrounded by tea and cake, seemed unreal to the soldiers on the front line.

All just cannon fodder, but here's a medal if you make it, all the same. During the war years the London horticulturists had their first flower show, aptly on the Royal Hospital grounds of Chelsea. They were the first to introduce and show off the plant hunters' findings from around the globe: dahlias from Mexico and chrysanthemums from Asia, along with the pungent musk roses of China, with the odd few foxgloves and prize veg. They set the bar in horticultural excellence for the growers and exhibitors, all with royal approval and nod, so from the dizzy heights of the London elite came the humble village shows around the country. Even our local villagers by the hillside were keen to mix their displays with the runner beans, fodder and the odd tuber chucked in for a bit of razzle dazzle. This harmless bit of competition would also set the scene for all prospective cottage garden growers within the villages up and down the country. The natural beauty of the natives didn't hold a light against the foreign contingent of flowers from warmer climes, which made the local meadow flowers feel a bit left out of the choice of posy on church days or the welcome home table display in the kitchen. The fuss and nurture it took to get to half the excellence of the finest growers in the land became an obsessive pastime, if only to beat Harry next door at the local village show.

So there we have the change in the post-war years into the roaring twenties, which meant that the native flower had no place in the neat rows of the staked dahlia canes. The only chance they had to shine was in the neglected space behind the potting shed, on which they would stealthily set their seed when the gardener wasn't watching and grow steadily amongst the Speedy Gonzales. They were referred to as weeds now, not wild herbs as in the previous century. The increase in medication and pills available also made the traditional methods of healing old hat and not a preferred practice for the educated young doctors and nurses.

Back home the casualties of war were praised and remembered for their bravery. The farmer's son and the lord's captain were equally shell-shocked and bruised by their experiences in the trenches. Post-traumatic stress disorder was undiagnosed amongst them all, with the repercussions felt in every household. Home and nature's way made them get back in the saddle, back into the fields or back onto the royal shoot. Alcohol for both acted as the best medicine to help them forget, but the medals awarded helped to give them courage when they looked for their lost foot or leg.

The hillside was totally unaware of the troubles abroad due to the war being fought on a different field. They noticed the increase in farming without the young lads guiding the plough, but they just thought it was due to them moving away to seek their own fortune. When they did return in their uniforms and crutches then the plants realised that it had been more than just a holiday away from the fields, and the construction of a stepped war memorial downstream also served to remind them of those who hadn't returned. And when the people picked the poppies from the field the following season the grief was reignited.

From this war came a wave of new machinery into the fields of the farmers, faster automobiles on the roads and a sharper suit amongst the nobles and landowners. The harvest celebrations still took place on the fields of the levels but with the introduction of new farmers' toys like a big red tractor driven by a large fella with a red face and welly boots just in case he had to get his feet dirty. The tractor saved a lot of time and labour, increased yields, didn't moan plus could get to most inclines of the land. Attachments would no doubt soon follow. The mechanisation of agriculture along with the advances in the automobile made the horse more and more redundant and often a hand-me-down to the poorer farmers down field, along with all the shackles and ploughs to boot. Horses were then considered old-fashioned and were nostalgically used for pleasurable jaunts across the fields and woods; the beer dray would hold on to the old traditions in the towns purely as a customary selling point to all the landlords en route. But as the world stepped on the gas so did the gases in the atmosphere slowly build, and the cities like London were obviously some of the first to add fuel to the fire. Keeping up with the Joneses meant the lucky few had a car and the best one could buy, although the horse guards parade was still present, along with the waving royal from the gold-plated carriages. That's just grounded tradition, I suppose?

As the chimneys still smoked and the car continued to choke the atmosphere, the unseen power stations on the outskirts of the large cities painted a bigger picture of the planet's problems. These came about due to the need for a thing called electricity, invented by the Victorians and widely used in the modern Edwardian homes across the country to mimic the static energy up until now experienced only in a scary thunderstorm. The fuel used to create electricity was … you guessed it, coal. By burning the coal you create steam, which drives a turbine which powers the electric coils. All waste went through a dirty great big chimney into the sky where it's somebody else's problem or in fact the future's problem, but hey, it doesn't matter – we are ignorant of all that at the moment, just keep the lights on please! I bet the dinosaurs are laughing in their reptile heaven, knowing that they have served us a legacy of disaster – revenge on all the future survivors they couldn't eat perhaps.

This warming of the planet gave the trees and plants faster growing times and increased productivity in their solar harvesters, but further downstream in the tropics and deserts the problem had only just begun. And to cap it all off the Arabs and the Americans had just realised they were sitting on a gold mine of oil with which to increase the planet's woes. Let battle commence over the cost of a barrel and we will build our cities in the sand.

Humanity's lazy streak

Humankind had always been dependent on something, be it the weather patterns to water their crops, the forests to circulate and absorb the pollutants, the shield of the ozone to protect them from harmful rays, or the car to get them from A to B. The slow walk to the shop or post office would be replaced by the powered scooter or car, and their routine of daily healthy activity was replaced by igniting the engine, a quick wave to the neighbour and I'm off to get my bread and butter. The humans' waistlines got larger due to their inability to use their legs, oh and can you do home delivery? You're probably getting my point.

Trees and plants, once again the forgotten link in the equation of life, are indeed the answer to all of this – the humans just don't realise it yet. If I had a time machine would my voice be heard back then as it would be heard today? I don't think so somehow. Even the great scientists of their time were being shunned due to the increase in corporate greed. A blessing was achieved, though, through the problems in the cities with smog and soot. The London plane was a hybrid of two trees (American sycamore/oriental plane) which were forced to live in the city to eventually become one tree through pollination. Recognised in France in the mid-nineteenth century, the hybrid had a remarkable ability to absorb all the pollutants into its leaves and particularly its bark, and a seasonal shedding would release the carbons into the ground naturally. It's funny how such a cosmopolitan city as Paris would be built on the combination of two different trees from two different continents solving one big problem. Soon these welcomed immigrants would be planted along all the roads of London, plus within the designated royal parks. This finding would make the humans start to realise that the trees and plants do have a purpose within modern society, especially if they help them out, but as we take two steps forward it's one step back, as the world catches up with itself.

The modern architecture of the time had embraced the Art Deco revolution. Out was the standard two up two down Edwardian terrace; in were the geometric squares of the art deco period, curves and all. A flat roof and clean lines, all coated in a neutral white or cream, was the beginning of the modernist architecture of present times, complete with its wooden floors and minimalist interiors. OCD cleanliness was to replace the old-fashioned good housekeeping of the polished step and battered carpet on the washing line. The garden also adopted this minimal fuss with straight lines of hedging all in a square patch of lawn. To add topiary or flowers would have been so dated, as they just wanted height and structure. The garage was the added bolt-on to these square homes.

In the suburbs the gardens were no longer used to produce food. All their owners needed to do was mow the lawn and sit and enjoy the cocktails of the weekend soirées. Don't get me wrong, this was a very niche few within the country, with the majority of the UK still living in the traditional stone cottage and Edwardian terrace, complete with the quintessentially common gardeners still growing their spuds and beans. The introduction of imported fruit and veg from the Americas and beyond made growing your own a hobby not a necessity for most of the middle classes. The poorer folk would be more reliant on feast or famine years; they would joke amongst themselves about the soft city-dwellers' approach to their manicured allotments. These more traditional hard-working gardeners were the salt of the earth. They, like their ancestors, had given the horticultural authors substance to write about: the best cure for blight or fly, or when to collect seed, sow and grow. Granted, most of the crop had been brought in from abroad over the centuries but like all plants and trees given a local name. Foraging in the woods and meadows was becoming a dying art.

The luxury of the local grocer began to make way for the cooperative groups of shops, and the combined strength of baker, butcher and grocer would pave the way for the supermarket. Their empires would be built on imports and world trade, plus put the squeeze on the local growers to produce more crops at a cheaper price. Now this was certain to put a strain on the plants of the world, wasn't it?

Modern farming

Back home the hillside saw the likes of the tractor replace the horse, and the car replace the cart. Less demand for limestone meant the slow-down of the quarry, probably because concrete was now the preference over lime as a standard building material. As the demands for bridge and road increased, plus for a quicker house-build, the eco-friendly, slow method of lime was replaced by the quick set cement. A sign of the times, I suppose. The eastern side of the wood jumped the road and continued to flourish up the coombe and beyond, and this part of the country saw no increase in development except for the expansion of the seaside towns around them. The arcades and seaside attractions were good for business, and the quarries producing cement were more productive due to local demand.

Quercus and co witnessed the expansion from the hilltop, along with the slow disappearance of the tribal hill forts which had been taken over by their distant cousins. The connection between the hill forts had been severed by humankind's growth, and the lack of communication between the trees of each fort meant that looking from one to the other was like viewing a distant planet. The trees also witnessed for the first time the invention of flight as it passed over their heads. They all stared in amazement as the ape became a bird, albeit a bit noisy from the single propped plane. It landed in the east past the coombe, and the trees could just make out a few faces peering out of the small windows. The birds laughed and said to themselves, 'It will never take off. Humans are meant to be on the ground.'

Very peacefully, one calm night, Quercus voiced his concerns to Fraxinus and Corylus. 'We have no purpose to the humans any more. The scientists seek our secrets but tend to be more interested in plants from far afield. The local tribes only want us when their coal runs low. We continue to soak up their problems and ask nothing in return. What is our purpose to them?'

Fraxinus agreed with Quercus: 'We are beginning to be the forgotten; we are all surplus to requirements. I so miss the interaction with humans. It's all getting a bit boring.'

Corylus, naturally the voice of reason, said, 'C'mon fellas, this is not the end of us. We are only just beginning to be recognised. Is it our fault the humans are too thick to realise it? I was only speaking to the ferns and fungi the other day about humankind, and their reply was simple – patience and understanding is the key to any success on this planet. Humans are barely a fingernail on the planet's history; they will naturally burn themselves out and we will just pick up the pieces.'

Quercus realised the ancient ferns were wiser than him, and he accepted their words as a kind of comfort but couldn't help feeling sorry for humankind, still just babies in the vast scale of things. Corylus also told them that a new wave of humans was starting to emerge. They were not driven by greed or the need to conquer but by caring for the planet in a kind of unelected caretaker's role. They were very few but growing in influence, and they sprang from the horticulturists of the big city. Their mission was to learn all about plants plus give their findings to the masses.

'How is that being achieved?' Fraxinus asked.

'Through books,' replied Corylus. 'It's not forced on people. It's more just for those who care to read.'

'Hang on,' said Quercus, 'weren't these the ones that brought us those invasive foreign plants along with those glass houses for the select few?'

'That's the ones,' Corylus said, 'but they are slowly coming around to our ideals and ways, along with people that not only care for plants but for animals too. It's all just a matter of time. We just have to try and convince the rest of the hillside that changes are afoot.'

The tapestry of plants within the wood and the meadow took this opportunity to give Corylus the benefit of the doubt, as they were in the front line of decline. The trees could stand tall and praise the humans but the plants, especially out in the meadows, were not so forgiving. They had no committee or freedom to choose to go where they pleased within the field boundaries created by humankind; their only loyal friendship was with the insects who jointly struggled to feed themselves. Their seasonal dalliances gave them a chance to catch up on the flowers far afield or at least within the radius of the insects' territory, and this network of pollination on the back of the bee determined who was faring the best in a kind of top ten. If you put aside the non-natives and concentrate on the locals, it was generally the big showy plants like the oxeye and scabious coming top, with buttercup and sorrel in close second and the orchids struggling in the lower ranks of the ten. Offset that against the early spring bulbs of wild garlic, bluebell and anemone and you had a regular food source until the clover and selfheal heralded the late autumn show. The insects could probably do with a bit more to harvest and store over the long cold winters, but like all living things they adapted to the availability. The plants just wished the humans would do the same instead of wasting so much when their granaries were full to the brim.

Second World War – make do and mend

The last world war had put a slight strain on the planet but the world was about to be really tested in a lesson of total war. As the warring tribes advanced further into mechanisation, with tank and bomber along with the machine gun and grenade, the scale of killing was doubled not only on the battlefields of Europe but also within the homes of the civilians. Britain was an island but was not safe from the German bombers of the Luftwaffe along with the submarines and battleships. The Third Reich under the dictator Adolf Hitler had a score to settle with the world. Britain was surrounded by the threat of invasion after the disastrous retreat of Dunkirk but also all supply routes of food and other commodities were severed by torpedoes hidden beneath the waves. This made the British people think about where they were going to get their food from, seeing that they had become dependent on imports from the USA for so long. Their usual self-sufficiency had been weakened by the cheaper crops abroad so they'd just failed to dig the ground, and suddenly all the people had to learn how to garden again through the 'Dig for Victory' campaign. There's the world thinking we were not only a nation of sea supremacy but also of gardeners, but in fact we were merely shopkeepers and yachtsmen who stepped in to rescue the desperate soldiers on the beaches of Normandy. This retreat gave the Germans reason to believe we were still fighting with spears and bows? The bottom line though was that the Navy was in retreat in order to save the fleet from a pending mass invasion. Just as well the Germans stopped at France and ate cheese and wine for a bit while they considered their next step.

All this threat of invasion gave the British tribes a chance to regroup and rethink for a short while. Well at least until the bombing started over the towns and cities of good old Blighty, but not to fear, we had the Spitfire and Hurricane to see off the Nazis in the aptly named Battle of Britain. These young tea-drinking heroes of the skies had both speed and manoeuvrability like a swarm of wasps to see off the squadrons of bombers, aided by a new technology called radar that would send out a pulse of radio waves high into the sky to be picked up by monitors on the ground like little dots. It's funny how such a technological breakthrough had been used by the bats of the world, including the ones seen on the hilltop most summer evenings, for thousands of years to guide their safe passage through a wood and field and to help them catch their prey. For their navigation system to be utilised in defence of the country – now there's something the bats could boast about to Quercus and co.

As the Germans built their bunkers and consolidated their defences along the French coastline, Hitler and his madmen concentrated their efforts on the Eastern front, giving the Brits a chance to re-arm and build more tanks, and when the Yanks joined the party due to the invasion of Pearl Harbor, the pressure eased slightly. The hilltop saw both friend and foe of the British in the sky, in the form of daylight training by the Air Force from their Mendip Hills base to the midnight bombing raids over Bristol, following the channel's moonlight runway. So as the night was ablaze over Bristol by the Luftwaffe's wrath, the hillside community could only imagine the terrible scenes of anguish and pain that both plant and human were enduring. Quercus said to his friends below, 'We can only watch and give pity. Our wood is always open to those who seek solace from the nightmares that lie ahead …' but as he was about to close his sentence the ground shook in what appeared to be multiple bomb drops within the coastal areas, as the planes offloaded their payload so as to conserve fuel for the journey home. Such was the spiteful way of war.

And like the war before this one, the young men were suited and booted for war, leaving an army of land girls to work the fields to provide for the increased need of food and supplies for a hungry population and marching army. Some young women were drafted in from the towns and cities, along with the young refugees of the blitzed cities, but they all contributed to getting the country fit and well for the uncertain future in front of them. Quercus laughed as the children of London had never seen a cow or sheep and never truly knew where their carrots and spuds came from – they just took all this for granted as mum and dad put it on a plate in front of them. They came to realise the hard work of producing the crops along with the harvest, and this life skill would indeed give them a useful leg up through their teenage and adult life; they just didn't know it yet.

They would also have to learn about the way of the land. With the pitfalls and joys throughout the war years, any question of why they were doing it was immediately put down to Hitler and his death army being defeated, not only on the battlefields but in the fields of food production – armies can't march on an empty stomach, you know. These same ideas were being carried out within the cities, as the dig for victory campaign gave the townies seed to grow their own crops, keep their own chickens and make do and mend. Any chance of an easy life was reserved by the privileged few or the spivs on the black market. A good contact was the storeman of the barracks plus the Yanks bringing over American treats like chocolate and stockings, gum and fags. The war brought a lot of pain and anguish along with unification and self-sufficiency, something the British people had lacked over the past hundred years, and this made them take stock of their environment and the plants around them. Suddenly the books written by the experts of the horticultural world gave knowledge and understanding, and things like nettle tea, jam preserves and foraging were a resurrected pastime, all embraced by the ladies of the WI right through to the scouts and guides.

With knowledge forgotten by humankind that had been second nature to their ancestors, the humans began to venture back into the woods where Quercus and co were standing, and they began to explore the possibilities of harvesting anything edible. The adults heard tales from their fathers that it's ok to pick the wild mushrooms but be careful of the colourful ones, it's ok to eat the fresh shoots of the ground elder, the wild strawberries are a free treat plus the sorrel and horseradish can spice up any Sunday roast. Some naturally got a belly ache and a bit sick from a glutty gorge due to their meagre daily ration. The flowers of the meadow gave the children a place to crawl and sneak up on the unsuspecting adult, mimicking a sniper in the field of conflict. Quercus and Fraxinus loved to see the children play amongst the cautious adults – an action and memory seen over many centuries and portrayed through many tribes. The children still had the same sense of play and devilment; their clothes were just not the same. Their playful antics would be abruptly stopped by a screeching pheasant lying low in the tall meadow grass, forcing them to hang on to mother's apron strings. Quercus said to his friends around him, 'Look, they are still learning and are equally as fragile as their cousins before them. Even though they have invented the tank and the gun, they're still weak amongst the wild.' Fraxinus agreed with Quercus and wondered if they were going backwards in their learning of the planet and the universe around them.

Corylus was paying no attention to either of them and continued to stare out over the levels. Her thoughts were of realisation and contemplation, probably due to spending too much time with the fungi and ferns (no reference to the hallucinogenic properties of the shroom). When she spoke, her words were of reason and understanding of humankind as she considered the neatly arranged patchwork quilt of fields all netted together by straight black roads bridging the rivers and streams. Her cousins were stranded alone but still alive and doing well along the tidy hedgerows and amongst the fields of corn and wheat. 'Humans are only improving on what the Romans gave them all those centuries ago and making it stronger and better,' she said. 'Yes, there have been some upsets along the way, and no one likes change, especially us trees and plants. But the meadows are still holding strong on the ridges and hedgerows not used by man – look, they're still there, giggling and laughing amongst themselves as they flower under the warm sun, little munchkins they are. The bees and butterflies are doing just fine within our local patch. They always want more and more due to their hardworking gene, but they just use what's in front of them. The shambolic tapestry is still weaving its way through the woods and into the back gardens of humankind; they are just a bit preoccupied with this current fighting to concern themselves with neatness within their backyards. The planes fly over us and the cars race by, but we can cope with the increased carbon in the sky just as long as the levels don't affect us too much. This is another turning point in the history of the hillside, so let's just enjoy today as we may not have a tomorrow, fellas.'

Fraxinus piped up and said, 'Wow, you have spent too much time with the fungi … But hey, your words are once again true and wise; just get back to work and start thinking about producing some nuts.' Corylus laughed at Fraxinus's old school mentality. 'Some things never change,' she said.

This minor blip on the universal chart would also serve to make the people make do and mend, and realise the need for warmth and the impor-tance of food – sacrifices they had to make so that the military machine could defeat a terrible enemy. If only they had known the true horrors of the war inflicted on the Jews through ethnic cleansing enforced by the Nazi rule. The villages and towns only processed the war in terms of government propaganda plus the number of bombs dropped on the cities. Hitler had to be stopped but to the Jews his war was personal, which made it so wrong compared to other wars. Such determination for defeating their enemy led the Nazi machine and scientists to create weapons never seen before on the planet, but which in some way brought a glimmer of hope for humanity. So when the doodlebugs were targeted at London, the world stopped and stared in disbelief; when the jet engine powered past the Spitfire in combat the pilots thought it was an alien invasion. And when the human guinea pig went under the knife by the doctors of the German medical corps under exposure to strong chemicals, the cures for certain diseases were found off the back of conflict. These mad professors worked on live prey, which made their Victorian predecessors seem very tame in comparison.

When the war ended due to so many countries joining together in one cause, their findings and secrets led to technologies not seen or heard of before, and as the warring countries fought over the land rights of a defeated Germany, the walls went up to divide their territories. The rush and scrabble to seek out the mad scientists and war criminals began. Then the unthinkable happened on the shores of the Japanese people when the atomic bomb was dropped on Hiroshima. Humans had invented a weapon that had the potential to totally destroy the planet, and their fate at this point was not decided by the stars but by their own hands. It took a second bomb on Nagasaki for the Second World War to finally end on a very poignant note: what the Manhattan guys had invented, ironically inspired by a German scientist called Einstein, would change the way humans perceived war. Hand to hand conflict would be replaced by missiles fired far away or dropped from planes high in the sky, making the guilty feel less conscientious about their killings.

The post-war boom (countdown T minus 21 years to my arrival)

From the moment humankind managed to split the atom and master fusion, they really didn't know what they were letting themselves in for. All of a sudden every country wanted new toys when it came to arming themselves with the ultimate deterrent against their future enemies. So when the iron curtain went up the world was truly divided. Despite not seeing any of the war on their own shores, the American people took all the credit for winning the war, with the Russians claiming that they were the driving force behind Germany's defeat, and democracy versus communism became the new battleground. Anything east of Berlin, in the wake of the Russian push, was controlled by the communists, and the West was controlled by democracy under the American flag.

At this point the American Dream was beginning to boom, especially as most of the European countries like Britain were indebted to them. The rise of the Cadillac guzzler along with the King burger and fries fuelled the American people into a new era of modern times. So as the cars tripled in number and the fields filled up with beef cattle along with the mass fields of wheat and barley on the once prairie plains of Oklahoma, the world got a lot faster and wider.

In Britain the remnants of the war left the country in near ruin and on the brink of a financial crash, and rationing went on for many years after the war just so the people could catch their breath after what had just happened. Back on the hillside, nothing had changed, except for the young lads who returned as men, like their grandfathers before them with stories and nightmares to tell to the sleepy villagers. The child refugees from the war stayed until their parents were able to pick them up and bring them home, but sadly not all homes were intact. Many of the refugees had been turned into orphans, but at least they had their enforced foster parents to hopefully look after them? The end of the war gave time for a party or two along with playtime for the kids. The hillside saw it as a welcoming breath of fresh air when the children played amongst their feet without a care in the world. Some of the more reserved kids, though, would just slightly smile as others ran down the steep slopes and tumbled into a pile of legs and arms. These snotty-nosed rag tag kids were the new hope for the country's future, and Quercus and his friends saw good in them, as all the conflict had made them tough kids that could take the hard knocks of life (sorry, not going into an *Annie* song). This ability to look after themselves reflected on the adults as well, as most of the people took nothing for granted and continued to make do and mend any broken tool or moth-eaten sock. Sunday play eventually turned to hard graft back on the fields of the levels for the youngsters, so when the Yanks left the seaside town they returned a decade later with rock 'n' roll and burgers to excite the teenagers of the fields.

The war gave the British people a hunger for success which spurred on their own ambitions and entrepreneurial goals, making them the landowners and business proprietors of the future. They would rebuild the country with bricks and mortar to help home the families of the refugees and orphans, along with factories – in this county – that made shoes, furniture and cream cakes to give them stable employment along with their council-built homes. Industry was beginning to reach the rural towns due to the rising population, which in turn made all the local economies boom, and with wealth came status and a better car to impress the neighbours with. The American lifestyle had begun to make its mark amongst the villagers near the hillside – the young farmers had their quiffs, but still knew how to steer a Massey Ferguson through a tight bend in the field.

Cuckoo Flower
Cardamine pratensis

Tufted Vetch
Vicia cracca

Meadow Cranesbill
Geranium pratense

This green and pleasant land: Post-war back to basics

T minus 10 years to my arrival

All this development and rush to build meant that nature couldn't keep up with the ever-bulging cities and towns, so as the green belt was designated and white land made way for industrial plots, the ecosystem struggled to adjust. Some animals did prosper under the build, like the nesting birds under a tiled roof, and the rural fox turned city dweller drawn to the increase in humans' food waste. These animals, like humans, are opportunists – give them food to eat and a convenient structure to live under and they will stay on until force is needed to evict them. The rise of the domestic cat and dopey dog gave the wild animals cause to worry, but they were cleverer than that. For years they had survived under the roof of the farmhouse and in the barns, so a few extra humans wouldn't deter them. This nonetheless turned the humans into believing that the wild animals were dirty and harnessed disease so they would have to go – just remember to close the lid on your bin and bring the pets' food in at night, hey? Oh, and stop feeding the birds with bread and chicken bones; that should stop 'em. No, instead we'll put rat poison down to kill them. That should do it, and when they return we will lace the boards with more. This ignorance towards nature led the competent rural youngsters into believing that all things could be treated by chemical warfare, so is it any wonder that the rivers and seas began to get polluted by our need for domestic cleanliness? The fifties saw the rise of the plastic revolution plus the rise in the soap suds and bleach: we have no time to scrub and stare when all around us people are drinking and dancing to the fast rock 'n' roll jive. Large chemical plants were built on the mouths of rivers to accommodate the ammonia-emitting chimneys along with the chemical plants of doom, and meanwhile slowly through little aerosol containers more poisons were unleashed around the country. All those beehive hairstyles would have had no staying power without them. There's me thinking the industrial revolution was bad!

The hillside groups noticed the acrid yellow plumes of smoke over what were once the quiet and clean fishing villages of the Bristol channel. Combined with the hotchpotch of chemicals already present, it polluted every street and every stream in its wake. The trees and plants knew they couldn't absorb it nor divert it, but just tolerate it. 'What are we to do, Quercus?' the little meadow plants asked, and his reply was swift. 'We can do nothing, my friends. We can only hope they will see sense in time.'

The chemical trend continued to grow within the psyche of the country so, as the farmers turned the soil and burned the stubble, replicating what was once a seasonal burn on the heathland, the planet began to warm up even more under its protective ozone layer. As it soaked up the large lakes of Africa like a giant sponge, the poles would begin to melt, gradually leading to rising sea levels. Not to worry, we have sun block and plenty of water in the reservoirs to see us into the next century. Just in case though, we will use the aerosol to keep us smelling fresh under the pressure of a hot day – as cool as Elvis with a neat quiff of hair. Someone had better tell the Brazilians that their country is keeping the air clean. Nah, we'll clear the forests to keep the Americans in coffee and burgers – after all, we have acres of land to exploit. This deforestation on a grand scale in the developing countries echoed Britain's medieval past. And Europe's too, it's just that no one knew the full extent of the problems they were creating.

Hot summers then turned to fierce winters in the early sixties. Well then, global warming isn't all so bad is it anyway?

The scientists had other concerns when the space race was in full swing. From the makings of the Second World War came the rockets which enabled humankind to break free of the planet's gravitational pull. Funny though that as we mastered the rocket the first to go up into space was a dog called Laika followed by a string of monkeys. Humans only went up after it was safe to do so … Well you didn't think they would try it out first without a few guinea pigs, did you! Satellites and machines were the first to send pictures back of Earth from space. The true beauty of the planet hadn't been realised on the ground – it took a photo from space to make human-kind realise its true hidden beauty. Seeing the planet from space or from a hilltop, the reaction is the same – you see the beauty but are ignorant of the arguments and troubles far away. All fluffy clouds, blue seas and green land-mass can trick the eye into thinking it's a wonderful world. Humankind, before we launch ourselves further into space to seek out new life and new civilisations, don't you think it might be a good idea to get our own house in order? Nope, we will continue to compete with our fellow human until we have reached the moon and beyond.

All this fast consumerism and the make-believe world seen in the cinemas and on the TV (well if you could afford one) was a far cry from the life of the villagers of the hillside. They were still adjusting to the fact that the war was over. A slow pace had been seen in the village up to now, save the busy market days plus the non-stop train from town to the cities. The increasing population, along with the developments of the seaside towns and the lack of adequate housing, created the rise of the council estate and switched the emphasis from agriculture to development to keep up with the demand. The village was no exception to the local council's demands and it wasn't long before circles of council homes were being built on the farmers' land, both north and south of the village. Built to home the less fortunate of the post-war years, the uneducated and the needy, and combining that with the invention of the NHS, you have the beginnings of a welfare state, all point scored by the elected governments of the time. The post-war years also left a huge skills gap amongst the people, especially as the need for new homes and new hospitals required more labourers. We as a country for centuries have welcomed migrant workers from around the globe to build our canals and railways, plus as cheap labour for the stately homes and gardens. Was the influx of the immigrants in the 50s and 60s any different than it had been previously? Apparently so, as amongst the British people were heard words like 'We fought for our country and get nothing in return – you give all the jobs to the immigrants.' The fact was they were willing to work and care for our sick, they were willing to put up or shut up, and to give their children a better start in life through schools and perhaps university. The war is over, so can we just get on with each other with one common goal? Instead of prejudice let's embrace change as planet people not as enemies like the Nazi regime.

Centuries of acceptance and tolerance amongst the hillside teams had made them a cosmopolitan lot. Granted, at first they never saw eye to eye but they learnt to get along and muck in together when things got tough, drink nitrogen and carry on. Humans are stubborn and hold on to too many grudges, meaning that sadly there is a race or creed that will eventually pay the highest price of all. Humans' chequered history has a bad habit of repeating itself.

The British people were divided once again in an undeclared civil rights debate, as the immigrants came flooding in off the boats from the Commonwealth countries. We'd conquered them a century or so earlier so to me it seems only fair that we should give them a home in exchange for their loyal support of the royal family. I'm in no way racist and hate to see or hear of racism towards our cousins, and I just wish everyone shared my view. If the Georgians hadn't capitalised on the slave trade, the native Africans would not have been put to work in the fields of the Caribbean, and if the Victorian imperial rule hadn't stretched to Asia then we wouldn't be arguing over providing passports to the loyal subjects of India. After all, we are all human and all bleed the same.

So, as the mass migration of the human kind continued, so did the steady flow of food from all four corners of the planet, along with all manner of plants and trees, from tulips from Amsterdam to petunias from South America. This influx of foreign plants influenced the way the typical British garden looked, but most plants of the day were born out of cultivated stock so had little or no pollen for the insects to feed on. Here lies the problem within the mindset of the British people in those early decades of the twentieth century and beyond. Bright, blousey, non-native blooms replaced the usual cottage garden favourites of wild herb and European herbs, which we as gardeners had given English names. Set that against the towering dahlias, trailing petunia and the lively marigold and you begin to have a garden that is not only unproductive but also totally unsustainable. By planting everything neatly standing to attention in rows, supported by a line of cane and string, humanity had mastered the growing of the non-natives within their chocolate box gardens, but they only knew neatness and formality because they lived in a world of squares and circles. The native wild herbs grew more freely in a randomly shambolic tapestry of plants, but humanity saw this as an unkempt mess, and felt the need to control the green spaces within the great parks of the country. Sadly, our loyal natives got pushed aside at this point, with humanity choosing only to slash and burn their growth until all appeared to have been destroyed. The native plants on the other hand knew that their day would come as soon as the gardens were neglected by the humans.

Every terraced street in the UK adopted this style of gardening throughout the summer months, in a collective 'Britain in Bloom' frenzy, each daring to be different and bolder each year; a collective mix which resembled a rich curry sauce leaving you with a sick tummy afterwards. Along with these annual foreigners came the greenhouse, which was a new addition to the British gardener's potting or home brew shed, which enabled gardeners to propagate and nurture the plants from the warmer climes despite the British frost – some heating their greenhouses with paraffin, others taking their chances with the sunshine. The horticulturists would teach them how and when to sow, along with the plants' pending weaknesses and diseases, oh and don't forget to protect them from the native snail or slug who from the wet meadows will make a beeline for them once established. A hundred and one ways were given for how to kill these unassuming invertebrates to stop them nibbling on the fleshy fresh shoots. God help the ones subjected to the midnight raids with the torch and salt. Ring any bells? Soon someone would invent the slug pellet to solve all of the gardener's woes against the enemy from the field.

Back home the meadow family had the opportunity to meet the foreigners within a local garden at the foot of the hill. Buttercup, already banned from the cabbage patch, was accompanied by sorrel along with fescue. They all peered over the hedge into the local prizewinning gardener's allotment. There lay the marigold amongst the cabbages, the nasturtiums amongst the Brussels sprouts. Buttercup would see how they fared over a couple of months. Sorrel posed the question of where so many aphids had come from. Hundreds more seemed to turn up when the vegetable crop replaced the meadow. Fescue stretched his blade to also see the marching snails from under the planks of wood heading towards the newly planted marigold. The plants all giggled to themselves and said, 'Well the gardener's got his work cut out this week! Shall we leave him be and wait until the autumn to spread our seed on the freshly dug soil?' 'Yeah,' the sorrel agreed, 'he's got enough on his plate.' 'Or not,' Buttercup replied. 'There's always the local supermarket.' All the plants agreed that it would probably take some time before the marigold and nasturtiums would be fully integrated into their tapestry of plants, and it would take at least until they had survived their first winter outdoors. The gardener, being none the wiser, was more interested in the voice of the nagging women wanting more flowers on the front path than he was concerned about a prospective autumn harvest. How times change so quickly from gardening being a necessity to becoming a hobby of pointless competition. Sustainable it is not. To provide for the whole family for a full year? No chance. Does it look pretty though? Even this is only a matter of opinion …

Glasshouses

Within the once boggy marshland of the levels adjacent to the river Yeo popped up many a large glasshouse to propagate and grow all the southern softy plants brought in from abroad. Their sole purpose was to give maximum colour annually for six months or more to the ever admiring local gardeners, who would cram them into a pot or basket with the finest compost they could make. Once sold to the public, their feeding, watering and nurturing were out of the growers' hands: '… just be careful of the late frost – they may just wilt and die. We have plenty more stock though if needed.' For me, the rise in the commercial growers' need to produce bedding out of season and force it out onto the public so soon cheated nature itself, and this along with the plants lacking any purpose or pollen for the local insects makes it all a bit of a waste of time. It wasn't too long before the annual invasion of bedding was preferred over the usual natural native display. Cowslip and primrose were swept aside for the more colourful cultivars produced under glass by the gene-splitting nursery growers. Gardeners around the hillside lost their way a bit from this day forward, as the nurseries provided their plants on a plate in their neat little plastic pots and trays. Whatever next? Perhaps an out of town mall or play area, or a flashy coffee shop? Well, perhaps in London. Gardeners are also not fools, especially the ones that grow their plants from the seed upwards. Their greatest reward is gained over years of nurture from the potting shed into the ground. But these gas heated glasshouses or plastic poly tunnels would accelerate all the fun out of growing a prize bloom or shrub, as suddenly they had the established plant available to buy without the need to grow it and wait. Yes, consumerism had made its way to the gardener via the fast-track temptation of quick gardening.

From the hillside, Quercus and the meadow teams watched patiently as these metal-framed glasshouses were being built, all with a slight reservation about their success, especially for the plants neatly lined up in rows on the raised tables. Around the back of the glasshouse the nettle and bramble were disturbed by all the building, but found themselves peering into the world of glasshouse neatness with their stems pressed hard against the glass. However, they were able not only to observe but also to take full advantage of the additional moisture and warmth generated by the glass, giving them the shelter and moisture to grow really well. To them it seemed so automated and false though, especially when they collectively heard the early seed crack out of season under the sweaty glass and plastic. The cowslip and primrose were all still asleep in stasis under a blanket of frost and snow, so at this point they didn't hear their distant cousins awake and punch out their stems followed by their squeak of leaf then loud shout of flower. My god they were loud, collectively under the echo of glass, and their bright colours would also amplify their voices amongst the early season daffodils and pansies. Quercus noticed with a bit of envy that they all grew so fast from seed. What if he'd had such a soft, fast upbringing – would he be any bigger or stronger now? The meadow buttercup would remind Quercus that the newcomers were not from these climes so they needed a bit more attention in our cold winters, and it was highly unlikely that they would survive into the next season. Quercus looked down and was saddened by that, as they looked like a fun lot to talk to and learn from.

So as the plants from the glasshouse took on strong root and flower following their weekly dose of chemical feed, they were ready to be placed on the wheeled trolleys and into the cooler shop displays. This is when the hillside crew never saw them again as they were bought and adopted by gardeners for their early front door displays. Like little children the plants all said goodbye to each other with an end of school wave, some from the warm window of the cars, others before they were lobbed in the boot or carried home in the cold February sun. Then just as soon as one plant was sold, more stock was being sown to keep up with the demand – more water, more heat and more feed needed. The bumble bee, curious about all the commotion surrounding the glasshouse, was drawn to all the bright colours within. A head-butt later from the glass meant his passage in was deflected away towards the hillside – a stroke of luck for some, while others wandered in through an open door only to be disappointed by the lack of pollen. Their escape was blocked by the closed door, and the buttercup saw the frantic actions of the bee as she continued to knock herself senseless against the glass until her fate was sealed by the daily paper of the nursery grower. Saddened by this, the meadow teams tried to warn all the other insects not to go in, but unfortunately for some the lure of the colour was too much to resist. If it wasn't the paper that got them, the choke of the spray and the humidity slowly ground them down. But even the plants within had their own problems to solve.

Some failed due to the lack of hygiene in their controlled state leading to powdery mildew and botrytis due to the high levels of humidity plus pour drainage amongst the crowded plants. Chemicals being their only saviour would be too late for some, while others would grow in a mangled state. The plastic trays full of diseased compost were disregarded behind the glasshouse into the cold, where the awaiting nettle and bramble absorbed all their nutrients, without the effects of the fungi. Their tunnelling roots were soon to invade the inner sanctum of the glasshouse floor. The meadow teams had a slight grievance towards the nettle and bramble due to them wanting to first take over the meadow and then the world, but even they all agreed that no plant should endure early death from a fungus driven by humankind's activity. 'Careful though,' they warned, 'the fungus will affect you as well if you go in there, so tread carefully if you wish to proceed into the warmth and out of the cold. Your invasion may have to wait …'. 'I don't think so,' replied the nettle.

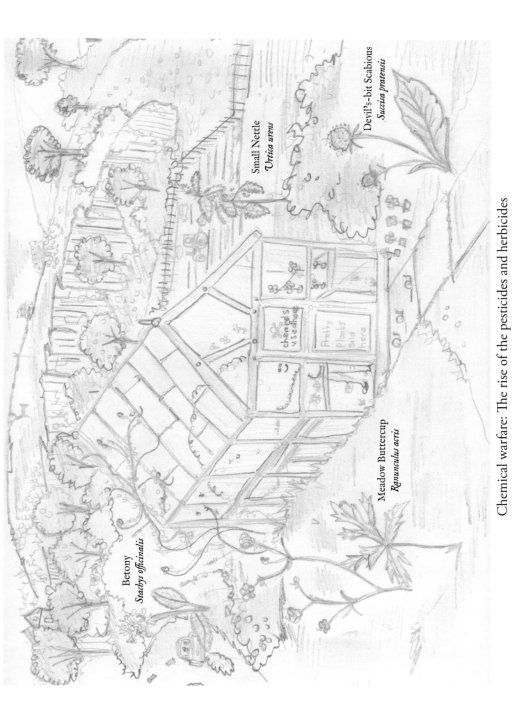

Small Nettle
Urtica urens

Devil's-bit Scabious
Succisa pratensis

chemicals used here

Pretty
Plants
sold
here

Meadow Buttercup
Ranunculus acris

Betony
Stachys officinalis

Chemical warfare: The rise of the pesticides and herbicides

As the dormant fungi lay in wait on the unclean floor they generated their asexual spores, which wrought havoc upon the poor plants in their path. The mushrooms and ferns on the hillside watched intently as their cousins took to the air within the warm glasshouse and settled down unsuspectedly on top of the fresh shoots of the primulas. The algae of the woods also watched this with great attention. Humankind had harnessed a new breed of fungus due to their need to control the plants' growth, even though the problem could be solved by sowing and growing the plants outside. Without a glasshouse the plant had the freedom of air circulation, a little bit of shade, ample drainage and root growth within the earth that it is born to live in. It wasn't the fault of the fungi that the plants died due to their activity. They were just capitalising on an ideal situation for them to grow in. Money and sympathy didn't really come into their equation of life.

Once the plants that survived the onslaught of the fungi were strong enough, they were hardened up to the outside world through a slow introduction to the climate, but once this was done it was down to the care of the buyers to do as they pleased with them. The horticulturists of London advised the growers to be more vigilant next time, with great tips on how to maximise their productivity leading to more glasshouses being built on the land. This act of growth in the wrong direction for a sustainable future was replicated all across the country, some growing flowers, others growing fruit and veg. By introducing vegetables from warmer climes into a world of control by humankind to supply and feed a hungry planet, heated gas-powered glasshouses could indeed prolong the growing season for a few more months but they were not the final solution. The increase in seed supplies though, by the companies that took time to harvest the next generation of plants (something the common gardener had done for decades through plant and seed share over the garden fence) was good news for the plants of the world. Not only was it a chance to secure ancient varieties out of fashion with the fickle growers, but by keeping seeds in deep stasis within the refrigerated vaults of London, we could ensure we had a food source pending a nuclear war. We could regrow after all the radiation had dispersed, and it would only take the odd hundred years to restart the chain of life! So as we continued to fuss, split and genetically adjust the linked cousins of plants to our own advantage, the hillside just continued its annual growth, shed and composting of the land.

The buttercup and sorrel looked at each other a bit bemused by it all, thinking, 'Is this the future of plants on the moor and the hillside or are we just not being heard by humankind?' Corylus said to the meadow group, 'Nah, it's just the way humans are adapting under the influence of the London showers and growers. We still have a voice amongst the insects and cattle, along with a few farmers wishing to enjoy our beauty on a warm spring day. Don't worry,' Corylus said, 'it's just a phase they're going through at the moment. They'll grow out of it.'

The north-side cottage was slightly different from all the surrounding houses. It had a sense of belonging even in its early days of development towards the end of the nineteenth century, nestled at the foot of the hillside but accessible by the ancient byway from the main road. Its great location gave the garden full sun along with deep shade and dappled shade from the surrounding woods. It was built, like most of the local cottages, with stone taken from the hill fort, with only the walls to separate human and plant. This small, compact cottage had no services and no connection to the world except running water provided by the Victorian pump house on the south side of the hill. The family enjoyed their pigs, their chickens and their large allotment on the undulating fertile soil to the north. I like to think they were the last remnants of a family that had lived and worked the hillside since the early days of the hill fort, but that's just me romancing the situation to my advantage. They were probably a local family from the moor wanting to get away from all the fuss in the local village to do as they pleased when they pleased, not to mention being close to the local pub on the hill. The meadow plants knew the family all too well as their adversary in the battle for land supremacy, but they tolerated the family's control of the shallow topsoil ridge to support their need for food within a twelve-month – it's just that they need so much to survive! The humans likewise tolerated the meadow plants, save the nettle and thistle that took a bit more persuasion to leave their patch of potato or beans. So the meadow clan just chose, as always, to go around the sides with the odd advance when conditions suited them. The family worked the land in an organic and sustainable way, and the buttercup, sorrel and fescue respected that due to a recent bad episode with chemicals on the neighbouring farmer's land. They only had to put up with the hoe and the spade with these people.

The family also saw the advantage of using the local resources for their crops, from the broken-down leaf mould in the lane to the potash in their wood burner, along with the trace elements of nutrients in the rock's substrate. They embraced the medieval ideas of leaving the wild herbs in the ground to draw up the minerals in a form of plant mining, only to be harnessed in the winter through the shallow plough. They also planted varieties that took little or no fuss to grow, like the spud and the runner bean. Their only secret was what the woods provided for them in the form of leaf mould, along with excess straw and grass to create a barrier of moisture retention. The chickens also provided dung once it was removed from the field. This was something the spud and the bean along with the cabbage and fruit needed in abundance, as replicated by nature's way of decomposition, unlike their glasshouse counterparts who relied on the squeezed chemical pellet and liquid feed to force on growth in their perfect warm conditions.

The pigs would also prove to test all of the woodland groups like the bluebell and wild garlic due to their ploughing snouts ripping up the ground to seek hidden mushrooms beneath. Their actions, like the chickens', would strip the land bare of all plants until their fate was sealed by the butcher for Sunday roast. Resting the land for a six-month would give the plants a chance to re-establish themselves for the next season of carnage by beak and snout, and this worked well for the humans too, as their need to maintain the land was reduced by the working farm animals, who also turned the land ready for the next seed drop. Fraxinus being the nearest tree to the pigs would serve as a great back scratcher plus shelter, much to the annoyance of the nearby celandine, cyclamen and primrose. They only wished the pigs would choose another area to trash and leave them to get on with their day to day business of seed dispersal and root growth. So they giggled amongst themselves one night and decided, as the sow was sleeping, or shall I say grunting and snoring, to place their seed on top of her so as to piggy back to the next part of the field, where she would naturally shake her back as the seed irritated her. 'We, my friends, will have freedom to roam and grow – we are victorious. It could be worse,' they said amongst themselves. 'It could be ivy or bramble taking hold amongst our soil – at least the pig waddles off from time to time.'

We have other pressing matters to attend to at the moment due to the rise in humankind's need for more food on a global scale.

Biological warfare

Back to the big deal, not only locally but regionally and even planetarily. Agriculture was the first skill created by humankind with which they were able to provide a crop to last a whole season, store it in a grain pit or granary, and make nice stuff like bread and beer. Now not a lot had changed since the early days of grain to the table and so on; what made it easy for the humans was first the ox, then horse power, but the crops still needed good sunlight, rainfall and fertile soil to grow. Simple, yeah? I'm afraid not. The increase in the world's population combined with its waste and greed only served to put a strain on the growing crops in the field, along with the increase in drought and insects (not wishing to blame the insects – they just eat and live off the back of an available food source). Drought is a universal problem and my assumption at this point is that by the mid-twentieth century it was down to human activity on the planet causing global warming, even if the Sahara was created long before a dirty engine was invented. The farmers in the field knew the benefits of spreading the proverbial cow manure on the fields to increase the soil's fertility. One tick to humanity. The medieval farmers had no machinery, just a hoe and a shovel to do the hard work of spreading the proverbial plus keeping the meadow invaders at bay by hand weeding. Some would even leave the weeds in the ground once the crop had grown enough height to be pollinated. The introduction of the tractor along with chemicals invented by humankind made it a lot easier for the farmer to do his job with a smaller workforce – who needs to hoe when we have a sprayer to bolt on to my tractor to kill all the unwanted weeds or indeed wild herbs?

So as arable farming increased, so naturally did the insects like caterpillars, aphids and wasps. Add the odd hundred thousand slugs and snails and you get a big problem on a large scale. The answer? Spray 'em out with a controlled pesticide and herbicide to not only kill the insects but keep the weeds at bay. Hang on, we eat the crops that are sprayed, so what does it mean to us? No questions asked from the unsuspecting supermarkets, and the farmer is only guided by the industry to what is in demand. I'm not going to tell you not to eat the crop as it's probably already passed through our system thousands of times since our own birth.

So when the field of barley was planted next to the hillside meadow all hell was let loose on planet Earth. One moment the meadow folk were enjoying an afternoon's giggle at the local farmer's string belt and moth eaten hat, the next thing they were being burned as they sat. If the atomic bomb was the problem of humankind, the spray of the tractor was equally as destructive to the plant world. As the bees passed by for a chat and a bit of pollen, suddenly they all fell from the sky, along with the butterfly and wasp. The farmer, unaware of their screams, simply rubbed his hands together singing country songs of a great harvest (no, not the Wurzels yet!).

Quercus and the hillside community could only hear and watch this carnage from far away, as suddenly a gust of wind took it towards them before it fell on even more unsuspecting ants and field mice below. As the dust settled and the full picture unfolded the only ones singing were the crops in the field. The buzzards high up took their chance to pick up the carrion as easy prey, but in time their fate would be sealed by the effect of the spray absorbed by their prey. To make matters worse, just as the large sprayer finished, the gardeners in their neat plots were spraying their roses with an equally bad killer, so the meadow family really didn't know which way to go.

My point from this is that up to the late 1950s into the mid 60s the chemical element was becoming as common as the Sunday roast or the daily pint of milk – it was widely used. Agriculture set the tone with the crops in the fields, which was copied and picked up by the horticultural growers and gardeners. No regulation was on the cards as hey, we are pest free with a neatly clean lawn and border. Happy days? Plants that were just sterile with no pollen gave the common gardener a lack of connection to the planet's tapestry of plants. It was chemical warfare not only in the fields of conflict but also on the fields of peace.

The 60s dawned to rapturous applause for the Beatles and the Mersey beat. These were just kids influenced by rock 'n' roll who did their gigs around the country to finally release a new sound that was liked by the Liverpudlians then liked by the world, wearing smart suits without a sniff of a quiff. Rock 'n' roll wasn't dead, this just sounded a bit different. The modern pop star was born off the back of screaming hysterical kids that had only previously seen their idols on the front of magazines and record sleeves. Other bands followed from the UK, which led the country into an invasion of all countries in peacetime Europe and beyond. Humankind still wanted to be held by the hand and loved by all who cared to admire them. Court jesters and famous composers had been replaced by the mop-heads. Teenagers were infatuated and the adults still had Frank Sinatra to swoon over.

By this time in the planet's history humankind had managed to create massive industries out of oil and the car with logos like Shell that contradicted their message a bit to the consumers at the fuel pumps. These oil companies along with the tobacco companies and fast food outlets were able to manipulate our reason to like them with glamorous advertising and TV commercials, with clean and crisp people smiling with their shiny new cars, or families around a table surrounded by burgers and chips. The rise of the canny advert slogan would also add appeal to the hidden dangers we were regularly inflicting on ourselves: don't worry, if it all gets a bit too much have a cigar and a beer to ease the day's problems. What they didn't say was do it in a responsible way, please. Like all human habits though, it's an inherent tendency passed down from centuries of ancestors who really only hoped to live into their 40s or maybe 50s, but that was old age back in medieval times. Humans had medicines to keep us going longer so that we could continue to abuse our planet and bodies until total organ failure ticked us off the growing population figures. Well at least until the baby boomers of the 50s and 60s came about, due to the rise in living standards and health care brought in by the British government. For those who didn't have a TV this meant more time to grow well, especially in my family. So there I did it, mentioned my lot. It was all meant to be a dramatic count-down to my pending arrival on this planet, but hey, I'm just going with the flow in my writing. I hope it's making a bit more sense now.

Nearly there

Before yours truly had arrived, the hillside was curiously watching over a group of humans with spades and clipboards dressed in baggy cords sporting shaggy beards – well that's my interpretation of an archaeologist in the 60s. Quercus and co were curious to see what they were up to as they marked out areas with pegs and string; they seemed to be concentrating on the hilltop. Corylus asked his hedgerow network to investigate what was going on, and the worry spread around the hillside due to the memory of a similar party some years back wanting to quarry the north side of the hill.

First to be dug up by the archaeologists were the wild flowers of cala-mint, scabious and rock rose, which had made their home in the south west corner on the rich fertile soil. Corylus reported back to her cous-ins with both apprehension and curiosity: 'It seems they are concentrating their efforts on the areas colonised by the ancient tribes of the hillside. No big earth movement, just little squares in which they sieve the soil through graded metal looking for items of interest.' Fraxinus replied, 'Don't they know what they're looking for? We know the hillside goes right back to the ancient tribes, so surely it's common knowledge that the remnants are here?' Quercus then replied with, 'Well perhaps they have forgotten their history due to their hurry to get nowhere in particular.' Always the voice of reason, Corylus said, 'Well it's nice to see that they are taking the time to find out about their past. Other tribes before them just wanted to destroy or blow it up. Who knows, they may even learn a thing or two about their distant cousins.'

Now this is where the whole space race thing puzzles me. Humankind still had a lot to learn from their past, along with the plants and trees, the animals and the elements present on planet Earth. Through military advances we get such good things along with so many bad things, but why oh why do we need to explore the universe so quickly when we haven't got our own house in order? The universe can wait and has had plenty of time to do so. Hurtling across space in our primitive machines is not going to earn us any more brownie points within the big scale of things. What really do we achieve other than bragging rights and land ownership? It doesn't mean diddly squat to be a conqueror if we don't make our planet a better place to live on. The hillside and the animals that live there are in their own small universe, but as a time machine has just been invented in the form of the dig, let's learn from our mistakes and move on.

It turned out though that the archaeologists found many treasures of tools and brooches used by the ancient tribes, a once forgotten civilisation that had lived and died there for many centuries. The local Roman temple remains were just a reminder that time had moved on for the hillside, so as the archaeologists filled in the holes and recorded their findings they all looked back over the moor and appreciated its beauty, some closing their eyes and listening to the birds and the rustling of the trees. The archaeologists had sought time travel and had found it in that split second of quiet, well at least until the noisy plane passed over their heads and the roar of the cars was heard as they sped along the roads. The hillside was only too happy to oblige them their bit of glory amongst others doing similar digs around the country, some finding the odd sword or armour, with others finding hoards of gold.

PART 5
MY CONNECTION TO THE HILLSIDE

May 28th 1968 – the arrival of twins

The time unknown, all I know is I arrived 20 minutes after my twin sister. I think they were going for an odd number of seven kids until I popped out unexpectedly. I also like to think the planets aligned and the universe was complete when I was born into this world, probably kicking and screaming and saying my god what's all this about then? Being the youngest of eight kids I was always going to be the runt, the last in the queue, the little teased one by my older brothers and sisters – that's how the cookie crumbled on my arrival. Like the forming of the planets and universe, Lady Luck shined on Earth and gave us light, eventually making my minuscule splidge on the timeline seem very insignificant compared to all the other millions born on that day. I was born into poverty but with the love of a family that would naturally keep me out of harm's way. Whether I liked it or not, the living and breathing dolls in the pram, me and my twin Jane, were to my older sisters a smelly arrival and an annoyance to my brothers. Feeding times were fun – not like the Waltons in any way, more of a scene from the Simpsons. Still we managed to shovel the food in well when we'd all mastered the spoon or fork. Funny though, I can't really remember us all sitting at a table together save the odd Christmas or birthday – not enough tables and chairs, more like laps and worktops. Growing up with the Walker tribe had its tough times, smelly socks and dirty laundry, but we stuck together. My parents were both from the Midlands which makes me half Brummy! After an industrial pay-off from a company that cost Mum one of her eyes, we migrated south to the City Road of Bristol and bought a large house which had been converted into a B&B. All a bit vague from my parents as to what happened, but a sudden downturn of fortune meant we ended up in Knowle West in a small council house. We were needy and needed a roof over our head so naturally got a home with all the other needy people struggling to make ends meet – brand new homes already tarnished by the inhabitants. Pot calling the kettle black, Mark!

You see my dad was a bit of a chancer – couldn't read or write and still had a bit of a quiff from the 50s. He was a product of the government's requirement to supply a home and feed him without him going out to work – just trying to break the family record of kids, child support, milk tokens, oh and with a bit of a chip on his shoulder towards coloured people. His family history very vague to us all, we never fully asked him the question about his parents or any brothers or sisters; there was just talk of an orphan child that had no one. That part of my own personal history unknown leads me to think that I have no connections to my ancestors' path – am I Roman, Saxon, Norman or a true Brit? So I'm one of the millions who also don't know, other than the privileged nobles and royals who hold a charter in their hands and paintings on the wall of a ruthless conqueror …

Mum on the other hand was born in a small village just outside Droitwich on a small cottage / farm. Hers was a church-going, loving family who worked the land and fed the chickens. Grandad drove the lorries in the war for the local air base, and grandmother kept a proper home. Seems perfect until Mum met Dad, then history just moved on for the sake of our family. All a bit hush hush, no questions asked, just rumours which don't piece together at all well. Her side gives me stability in my past through my cousins and aunts and uncles firmly held in the Midlands. Does this mean I am a Viking or a Celtic Dobunni tribe member? Ho hum, let's get back to writing.

All I know is that my dad was a bit of a wanderer, never happy where he sat, never at home, except on Saturday afternoons for the wrestling and pools, and Sunday for the roast. It wasn't too long before we outgrew our home in Bristol and moved to a cottage in Cleeve, North Somerset – getting a bit closer to our hill fort friends, but far enough away for it to not fully matter to me at the mo. I must have been still a toddler at this point, living in a cottage built for the workers of the local estates or perhaps an influential farming family within the locale. Stone walls, tiled roof, a bit damp and smelly especially in the winter when the pipes froze and the coal fire choked the rooms due to an unclean chimney. Aah, but we were happy (a Monty Python sketch springs to mind). Our legacy was left some years later by the graffiti drawn on the walls by my family.

Early days

Vague like all things in my early life on this planet, my earliest memories were of our large council house in our beloved village on the moor, where we moved when I was five. It was built by the government to again provide homes not only for the farm workers but also for the workers at the factories within the village. The earlier tribes of the village were still embedded into the history of the area through the churchyards and street names and probably in the Domesday Book. I turn up none the wiser, just still dribbling with a snotty nose, clothed in my brothers' hand-me-downs and always in a high chair to save space on the floor. The youngest of us (me included) slept in cramped cradles and shared beds, and everybody just kept on growing. Too young to be a hippy, just in time to be a rug rat and a nuisance to my older sisters who cared for me when Mum had to go to work for a bit of spare cash.

With the summer of love a distant fading bloom and the Vietnam war a recurring nightmare for the Americans, the world seemed to change its smart suits to flares and large collars. Born out of the 60s were the 30-something would-be green warriors of the planet, whose anti-war slogans and rallies drove their stifled ideals as they drove their Ford Escorts to the office block in their baggy suits. They felt a longing to do what's right for the planet, forming Greenpeace and other environmental groups. Slowly but surely they managed to scrabble up enough money to make the odd leaflet and hold the odd jumble sale to help raise funding to teach the people of their wrongdoings on the planet. Like the hippies in the 60s they spent a lot of time outdoors enjoying what nature provided them with, including perhaps the odd festival next to an old tor in Somerset. Never washed, never shaved, body a temple … Yeah right, if they were transported back in time they would blend in well at any medieval market of the time. Their intentions though were good, marching against the wars and living organically and chemical-free except for the substances they inhaled! Suddenly the world had a conscience as to what it was doing to the planet, and the beginnings of a switch from greed and destruction to how we can help make it better for all of us. They were giving the animals and plants a voice amongst the politicians and corporate machines. Everything about the way we lived in the modern world was put under the microscope, from the pollution of the seas to the rising use of chemicals on the ground, plus the amount of pollutants chucked into the atmosphere. And all this kicking off before I had a chance to read my first Ladybird book. Knowing that I was born in an era of care and concern for the planet helped to shape my future, and along with being brought up in a village close to the hillside of Quercus and co, makes me feel special. I could have so easily been a proper townie in Bristol with more of a Hartcliffe tinge to my Somerset tones. Or a stout Brummy supporting the Villa or the Baggies and driving a milk float because I liked the electric hum and hated the diesel choke.

My dad a gardener, my mum a cleaner, we were stereotypical of our position in society: eight kids all in need of housing, feeding and teaching. Perhaps my life would have been different if I'd been born as a single child, spoilt with chocolate always on my face, but no, the stars granted me a large family with a tendency to fight and argue a lot. Still at least my upbringing connected me up with similar families within my street, some sharing their action men and go carts to the unfortunates, others greedily keeping their toys close to their chests and boasting about them. Divisions were made in those early days but hey, we were just kids; learning curves and life skills start at an early age in a rough community.

Suddenly the once rare one-car family had moved to a two-car family within the village, but parking problems at this point weren't an issue on the streets, and we as kids had time to play marbles and chalk up hopscotch in a street largely lacking the automobile. Each year, however, the latest model of car replaced last year's, causing a surplus of cheap second-hand cars, which led to the rise of clogged streets. To think that in the 70s a brand new Mini would cost an average of £600, with the average wage £32 a week, and bread at 9p – happy days then. We never had a telly until the mid-70s so never grew up with all the early stuff like the *Flower Pot Men*, *Andy Pandy* and *Muffin the Mule*. For the adults, *Gardeners' World* was aptly launched in the year before my birth to entertain the veteran gardener along with the unconverted willing to watch and learn. Prompted by a group of like-minded researchers the stars of the TV would transform a seed tray into a mass of colour or vegetables, oh and don't forget how to kill the unwanted and manipulate their growth. Educating the people about plants had just gone global all in a very twee way. How to split, divide, propagate and finely tune your perennial, lift and store your dahlia and double dig the old fashioned way – try telling my dad all this? This gave the other kids a good head start over me in the technologies and world around us. I just used my imagination when playing in the garden: no flowers, just high gutsy rye grass to roll around in. I'm sure that's why Dad never cut it, due to the tribal roll and stomp of the family beating it down to submission, the council chain-link fence keeping us in check, away from the world outside.

This once open farmland was home to the meadow friends on the hillside, their seed, which had been turned by the plough and tractor, only to be replaced by concrete and brick. I suspect the rye was seeded by the builder as a quick grower on the top of a sparsely top-soiled and rub-ble-filled garden, and his bag probably did the whole estate in one hit. No trees were replanted except, a bit later, a token effort of privet or lonicera hedge to mark the families' garden boundaries, all grown in a nursery in the Midlands I suspect. Still the benefit of the large sword of rye grass was that you could make the grass sing and talk if you held the blade between two thumbs and blew. The rye grass was happy for her voice to be amplified amongst all her cousins, along with her thick seed heads being pulled up between finger and thumb, dispersing her further afield. Mud on our shoes and seed in our hair made us the rough and tough kids we were until we came across a nettle or thorn. Then we were only too sure to change our opinion about plants when our hands itched and bled. No lessons came from our parents, just get out there and learn it yourself, find your natu-ral balance and walk on. All these early experiences made me wary of the plants around me along with all the bugs – watch out for the spider and be careful not to anger a bee. My ignorance as a child, along with no education on the workings of the planet, made me like most of the kids in my street: feeling the need to destroy what we didn't understand. Harsh it all seems now but hey, we were just kids.

The hillside at this point wasn't even on my radar; I was just in my own bubblegum and liquorice laces world of all the sweet things life could throw at me. The local corner shop was my Mecca on the way to school. I was too small to reach the counter but tall enough to see the glass jars of loveliness amongst the fags and newspapers. Like millions of children before me, the lure of the sugar-filled sweets made them my stable food source at break times, along with our free pint of milk. Potato and spam was our other reg-ular food source, if we were lucky with a dollop of Tommy K, and a knob of butter, a real treat – is the war still on? Vegetables came in the form of cheap cabbage and peas, and given that we didn't have a fridge, everything was perishable and not wasted on our table. As a kid, like all kids, to have a tasteless soggy piece of cabbage on your plate with a fish finger offered two choices: quickly eat the fish finger before being forced to eat your greens, or suffer the greens first and then enjoy the fish finger. Knowing the ben-efits of plants to me and my digestive system would have saved me a lot of tummy ache and fillings, but in all things temptations are put in front of you driven by your friends and peers. That cabbage had been carefully grown by the farmer in his muddy field, and being local and cheaply grown meant it was chemical free and probably sold at half its original size due to its caterpillar-eaten outer leaves being disregarded and given to the pigs before it went on sale at the local greengrocer's. Its sole purpose was to be on my plate for me to enjoy its hard work … not. How ungrateful was I? Now, where's my mint imperials? Ah, probably glued between the seats of the sofa, so foraging I go for treasures.

All my past writings of the tribes etc are now beginning to fall into place on a local level. My dad and mum worked for the wealthy landowners in the village, who, like the previous tribal leaders, had their followers and workers: some there out of necessity, others through loyalty. Being foreigners from Bristol/Brum, our ancestry had yet to be recorded in the local records, our position in the village to be confirmed by the locals along with any purpose or memories. So our history there hasn't been written – only the early forging of friendships in the playground of our local infant school, where my good friend Rob was first to 'break bread' with me with his apple core. This was in no way a reference to my need to be fed or showing any prejudice of status, just the start of a friendship due to us both agreeing I would have his apple core. He would seek me out in the playground through the bullies and the pigtails to give me his present of friendship. To this day it's a fond memory, sharing of germs and all that, like the native Americans through blood brothers. Well it didn't do us any harm anyway.

The age of learning

My local primary school gave me a purpose in the village. It had adults that were willing to teach me to read and write and to encourage my inner skills in the arts: some of us have hidden skills like drawing and singing that need to be nurtured, like a plant has to be nourished and nurtured to full bloom. A plant is like a human in a way, because its genetics hold the key to its success. Quercus on the hillside, along with Fraxinus and Corylus, had a strong gene to make him push up high and out-compete his rivals for light, moisture and nourishment. The other trees along the lower ridges, given their position, could never reach the height of Quercus and moaned that their status wasn't equal. The same beginnings are found in the playgrounds of infant schools. I consider myself on a par with Quercus and co because I had no help or assistance from my family on the path to my future. Other kids on the block had parents who taught them to read and write before school, giving them an advantage over their classmates on the early Ladybird books. I wasn't illiterate or stupid, just not nurtured earlier due to my dad's lack of education and my mum's busy schedule of laundry, cooking and cleaning for our small tribe of reprobates. So when we moved to a larger house north of the village and into the primary school, my need to learn became more and more important. The brainy Ladybird kids were just kids like me with all the same early problems like fitting in and being liked.

My childhood, like most people's, was a mixture of blurry moments followed by embedded lasting memories, like the smell of fresh paint and the echo of a wooden floor when we all viewed our new home in the street that we knew as the circle; new bedrooms to argue over along with the usual rota of washing days and feeding times. I knew from that stage I was on my own as most of my friends were on the south side of the village, but at least I had my brothers and sisters to tease me and keep me busy. Our garden was similar to the previous one – all grass, a hedge and a concrete path. Not a great start for a budding gardener to aspire to?

Looking back now, our small estate was probably once part of the nearby Masonic lodge, where strange things happened in the dead of the night! The nearby posh Edwardian homes had apple trees in the back gardens so my assumption is that when the council bought the land it was part of an orchard or indeed a meadow. The building site next to our street was probably owned by the wealthy landowner as well, as the need for homes outweighed the need for apples and pears, well at the right price of course. The village's expansion was driven by the needs of the local populace. The farmers had once lived on the outskirts of the village, but as new homes were built they became the centre of the village, as even their land was penned in by development. The network of meadows and trees was all gone save the odd large sycamore or willow, as the tapestry of natives had been ripped up and placed elsewhere to re-seed within the farmers' spoil heaps. Their journey back home would be dogged with tarmac and concrete.

Our home boasted a shrubby honeysuckle, privet hedge, oh and a gooseberry bush. What were the council thinking when they supplied us with food? The rear garden backed onto a dark lane called the Boards, and a rusty galvanised shed that smelled like something had died in it. Yuk! A cycle of trends from the previous house appeared on our dad's annual garden rota, ie spuds and long grass. Everything else was wild abandonment in the Walker household. Butterbur hogged the footpaths, along with neighbouring fruit trees undisturbed by any development, which tells me now something of the past history of the ground. The Boards, lined with hawthorn and hazel, links my story with Corylus's network of friends on the hillside, with the hint that the lane had been a boundary or drainage ditch due to the present butterbur, and who knows, perhaps the area had been a woodland, given the presence of the gooseberry in the garden? It's a question I ask now due to my ignorance back then as a child. Rest assured though, my network of hillside friends are beginning to introduce themselves.

Welcome to the hillside, Mark

Not sure how our first field trip out of the classroom came about and why the teachers got all outdoorsy and green, but they were probably ex-hippies longing for a fix of the good life? Needless to say, we all went hand in hand up the high street in our wellies and shorts and a heavy duffle coat, up to the hillside past the cricket club and into the woods. Without a sniff of a high viz or clipboard we were told we were going on a field trip to collect leaves. Now what did Quercus and co think of this when they saw a human chain of scruffy little urchins heading towards them? Corylus's hillside scouts followed us all up through the field, with on the left the quarry, on the right the large Georgian house. I wasn't aware of the eyes beaming down on me and my classmates, but as the autumn wind blew, Corylus shook off a few leaves which landed at my feet along with the odd cobnut. Fraxinus launched his helicopter seed heads in a shower over another group of kids while Quercus gently threw some acorns down. This gave the teachers something to inspire the kids with, and as we all handled nature's simple pleasures, they told us that like from small acorns we grow, and taught us how to forage and the importance of the trees around us. Never had the hillside teams seen such an enlightening insight into the young minds of humankind. They had witnessed both good and bad, but this brought a little tear of sap to their trunks. Us kids just liked the mud and puddles along with the outside air. Some kids were wrapped up in cotton wool and mollycoddled by the teacher, others stung by nettles in a symphony of wails and screams. I on the other hand felt right at home. Having no socks in my wellies made me feel primitive amongst the ancients, and a little bit of mud and stinging wouldn't deter me from enjoying myself.

We were not there that long due to the teachers wanting to return to their unscheduled coffee and fag break in the staff room. I remember returning though with a handful of leaves and seeds to display and press back in class. Books also taught me the leaf shapes and sizes, along with the Latin names of our native trees. It went in one ear and out the other, but subliminally I took it all on board in my memory banks. Other field trips followed when the weather was kind, where we pressed daisies, made daisy chains and checked if we liked butter from the shine of the buttercup's flower under our chins. Naturally we all liked butter except the ones who had dirty faces on the day, but a little bit of weekly soap and water would convince them that butter was best. It's funny how our meadow cousins were connected to us in our previous generations through folklore and superstitions, from way back when a Chinese whisper of good or bad had made our ancestors imagine and dream up new stories for the next generation of young thinkers. Buttercup, along with sorrel and fescue, were present in our playing field on sports days, play days and the days we want to forget. They as a collective were as much a part of school as books and dinners. We just took it all for granted.

As the 70s bounced on with the orange space hopper and moon dust sweets, my recollections of primary school are filled with memories not only of exploring the hillside but of the school concerts of *Jacob* and *Oliver Twist*, along with melting tarmac on the hot summer days as I walked back from school. Winters were equally as extreme with snowdrifts and food shortages – well no change with the food then, but my point is that we had such extremes of weather patterns, unlike today's mild winters and floods and storms.

Simple solutions like the metal tray and fertiliser bag would serve as our sledges on the steepest slope of the hillside, at a mass community event organised by no one in particular; we just all knew the best place to go on the north ridge. The bracken underneath was frozen and iced, and became the first layer on which a thick layer of snow would make the perfect piste. No one really had skies or top class sledges, just the best item the kitchen or garage could provide – a collection of junk that we all observed and took note of for the next day's best ride down the icy slope. Naturally there were casualties when people collided in this disorganised community event, a soft landing though was guaranteed where the virgin snow lay. Quercus and co loved to watch the fun going on down the slope, as not much else happened on the hillside in the cold winter months. The bracken, though, was not so pleased to have all this compression and sliding on his head, and he wished his home was on the south side, undisturbed and free from humans. Quercus with a restrained smile said, 'It's only a bit of fun; you'll bounce back in the spring to wreak havoc over the poor little orchids wishing to make good ground around you.' The bracken snuffled under the snow saying, 'It's not fair, the meadow folk don't have to put up with it so why should I?' Geography, my friend. That's all it is.

Well just as winter passed spring slowly appeared, to warm the hillside with little or no trace of all the fun of the winter, save the odd abandoned plank of wood and perhaps the odd bin bag and tray; OK, rubbish everywhere in the bushes under the trees. A fitting scene to end the winter of discontent amongst the striking workers of the country where poor pay and unions' voices had put a stranglehold onto the country's services, from the bin men to the fire brigade, oh and the rising miners and trade unions. The government had a hard job to control their angry demands for equal pay and equal rights for all brothers, as the workers united with the common goal of complete closure of the country. Deprivation and despair within the suburbs built by the architects of perfect living in the 50s and 60s just made the concrete carbuncles a boiling pot of troubles for the unemployed and elderly. Moving out of the slums and bomb-damaged homes into this modern day utopia back then gave the state the opportunity to lump all the underprivileged people together, out of the way, but the people, not stupid, caught on to what they were doing, woke up and rebelled like a group of marauding Vikings. No future, no past, they thought, just a tough outlook on life which made way for the anti-establishment movement of anarchistic music called punk. While the middle class was enjoying the likes of Abba and the Bee Gees, the youngsters were beginning to play a few chords on a guitar fuelled with all their pent-up anger within. No melody, no particular verse, just raging anger and swearing against the status quo … (not the rock band).

Back in the countryside, our village (what a nice thing to say, 'our village') was hidden and well away from all the fuss and fighting within the cities of the UK. Like all things explained so far in this story, the village was worlds apart from all the tension and wrangling, but the news was broadcast and in the daily paper and was chewed over by the locals. I can't remember the milk not being delivered to the doorstep, the bins not being emptied or stacking up, and even the coal got delivered on time. Our bubble of existence within the village was indeed worlds apart. The only thing that reached us was the music of the time, plus the second-hand fashion at the jumble sales. The back of beyond was our place in the country. People came and went and restocked the homes, and history is then rewritten. Punk came to me like most things in our household through the antics of my older brothers and sisters. I personally still liked the sounds of Abba but

I had an image to uphold amongst my friends and peers. Hanging out at the village shopping precinct along with the discos at the rugby club gave me mixed messages of the preferred choice of music. I heard mostly hippy rock or saw headbanging teenagers who appeared to me to be grown-ups because they drank beer and smoked funny fags. We hung out with the empties in the back yard, soaking up the foam from the beer barrels with a big stick and a cup, briefly looking in through the doors to see the psychedelic moving paisley patterns projected on the wall and spaced out older teenagers. They were probably only 14 or 15 but to me they came across as bordering on adulthood due to their size and bad habits. This collection of kids was probably no different to all the past teenagers within the village, with their parents equally as rebellious. Their futures were already worked out by the caring parent, be it to work the fields or in the local factories.

Our house had been built in the 50s but many more were built in the 60s and there was a further collection of building sites around our once quiet country lanes. For us the building sites were a place to play and get up to no good, some playing house, others playing more adult games amongst the incomplete semis. Lack of health and safety concerns meant that in the evenings and weekends we had the freedom to play war games with our neighbouring street, missiles of mud and stone launched over the farmer's boundary hedges. These almost tribal actions built loyalty and friendship within our street, and it wasn't too long before we started playing footie in the circle and jumping over the garden hedges like our own version of the grand national.

While my world was being moulded around me, the rest of the planet was experiencing a major change. With the rise of the fast food giants, fast cars and slow progress towards resolving the Cold War, humankind was quite happily burning the fossil fuels, and burning the midnight oil – all contributing to a fast pace of life. Environmental groups like Greenpeace were making their mark on the high seas as eco-pirates to the whaling trade and the oil giants, whilst vivisection warriors were knocking on the doors of the science labs.

A lighter form of environmental group turned up on the hillside one sunny Sunday. Drunk on the unrefined scrumpy of the local zider farm, both male and female frolicked and flirted on a post-dated summer of love frenzy. They were harmless enough and naturally got the attention of all the trees and plants of the hillside. Like their ancestors before them they congregated in a circle amongst one of the ancient roundhouses clearly visible on the hillside's meadow clearings. Quercus noticed some were humming, others were swaying and one bloke went positively green in colour. Fraxinus remarked jokingly, 'Look, they are taking root and filling up with chlorophyll!' A violent interruption of fluids from this chap soon afterwards meant their ritual-like chain was broken. Corylus was quick to mention that I suspect it was too many apples in his diet? They all staggered away in an unceremonious fashion, some tripping over, others looking quite disoriented. They sought shade from the midday sun and promptly headed straight towards Quercus, where they all marvelled at his height and girth and began to question his age. One male decided to reach his arms around Quercus but failed to get his fingers to touch. Then one of the females decided to link up her hands with his from the other side, which ended up being an early form of tree hug. Quercus had never experienced this before and was touched by their warmth. He felt their heartbeats within their fragile bodies and was quite moved. Fraxinus and Corylus also felt his emotions and were equally pleased by the experience. A respect and trust was gained on that day by both sides. But the humans' thirst for progress showed no sign of slowing.

So as the tarmac roads around the cities and towns got wider to ease the congestion, the air traffic increased as the jumbo jet and Concorde became the preferred travel option over train or boat. With all this commotion, the trees and plants tried to keep up with the pace, but when they were facing the digger and the dozer their progress ground almost to a halt. Thankfully there was no such push for progress on our hillside, so when the blasting stopped in the quarry a huge sigh of relief was heard amongst all the community, both plant and human. The lorries stopped hauling, along with the constant rumble of the stone conveyor belt. No dust, no noise, just peace and quiet; humanity's progress halted. The quarry had spent all its iron and ochre, and cheaper imports from abroad would soon see the industry within the country grind to a halt. Like the great power houses of Sheffield and Wales, where the industry had been a lifeblood to all, all that would be left were empty warehouses and full working men's clubs – good men wanting to work but knowing only one skill in the foundries and steel depots.

In time, nature would replace the abandoned industrial buildings with homes for the birds and insects, and as on the hillside the buddleia would be waiting in the wings to colonise the pavements and roads. Aerial attacks would be provided by the birds and wind to help establish its roots in the moss-filled gutters. The tapestry of plants would then slowly cover the roads, once heavily laden with constant traffic. Their statement to humanity is that if you don't use it, we will; just look how fast we can reclaim it. The areas in deep shade and the oiled floors would be left to collect dust and fester with only the footprints of the rats and foxes present – they unlike the plants are opportunist hunters that will quite happily live on humankind's disregarded scraps. This would be mirrored on the abandoned quarry of the hillside, with all the echoes of industry still present but in some way more peaceful and serene. The impact on the local economy was negligible due to the small size of the workforce, some of whom went off blasting other hills on the Mendips, while others drove the dozers and diggers in the local concrete plants. Waiting in the wings on this hillside were the forest fellas.

The hillside committee was gathered on the edge of the quarry and, faces up against the chain-link fence, they looked down to a massive chasm of nothingness. Not since the forming of the planet had they all witnessed so much open rock. This cross section of rock, subsoil and then topsoil reminded them of their life's struggle to root and grow. Some small trees could be seen hanging on for dear life on the edge of the quarry shelf, their roots twisted in mid air – a reprieve had been granted to them as the last stick of dynamite was lit. It may take thousands of years to rebuild the top soil layer for the meadow folk to colonise first but hey, we are going nowhere in a hurry. Gangs of nettle and bramble had already made the first invasion up and over the chain-link, sending out their lateral roots into any soil suitable to grow in, along with their aerial roots arching over the chasm in a wave of hope of reaching the bottom. Ivy, their arch rival, could be seen at the base working upwards. Her progress would be more productive given the pockets of soil that had drained down through the substrate. In some way they all silently cheered on their foes with a mark of respect to all the plants on the hillside. There was talk on the wind amongst the trees of a group of people that was establishing a woodland trust. What's this, you may ask? Humans planting trees for the sake of planting trees …? Unthinkable. But yes, it was happening. Suddenly motorway verges and fields were being planted up with trees, and seed collected, all in the name of preserving what was once green. All a bit of fun for the unfit office dwellers to enjoy at the weekend along with the odd school. There were no such schemes on the hillside though, which remained a playground for us all.

Like many of the kids from the village, I used to squeeze through the broken chain-link fence and play in the abandoned quarry full of man toys like rusty cranes and dozers. There were sheds full of metal and wood, their purpose unknown to us – we just wanted to get the diggers going. However, no fuel and flat batteries meant we had to just imagine a day's work behind those steel beasts. Some kids sought out the explosives shed, others threw stones at the foreman's window in an act of defiance towards his angry tones on our previous visits. The quarry was the first industry to fall within the village, but others would soon follow. We didn't mind because we were kids and enjoying it while it lasted. There was talk of a tip or landfill in due course.

Suddenly my weekly duty was to walk our dog Pupsy on a Sunday morning along with his newfound friend Murphy from the big house on the hill. Dad used to work there, and as I was passing, Murphy used to come along for the ride. Two powerful dogs, one skinny little urchin; still it made me stronger as time passed by. The obvious point of destination was the woodland hillside due to my independence at a very early age and the rare walks there with my dad. It seemed the right place to go. Any memories of the school trip had disappeared in my humdrum life with a stressed-out mum and fighting siblings. My trips to the hillside gave me space to breathe and forget about the trivial kid stuff and focus instead on making my dog happy on his weekly run, where I would let Pupsy off the lead and not see him for ages until out popped a rabbit with him on its tail. My youth held no responsibilities, especially where my dog was concerned. Adults would prefer to keep their hounds on a lead, but I just let the mutts get on with it. Dogs of the world sort out their differences through scent and smell, along with their eyes and their teeth.

Quercus and co were present throughout my childhood; I just didn't realise it back then. This was when I was unaware of the hillside's history and its previous inhabitants, along with the trials and tribulations they'd all had to endure. I, like the many walkers of the hillside, took it all for granted, only choosing to make up mad ideas like witches' cottages and the 'Devil's Steps', which was actually just a rock face for adventurous kids to play on. To be fair, though, I did take some of it in during my weekly walks with Pupsy – things like the deep hue of bluebell on the early spring woodland floor, the ferns unfurling amongst the leaf mould plus the heavy rock under my feet. The hillside family followed me on my journeys up to the encampment and back down again, I just wasn't ready to see or hear it in my small world. Perhaps I was hungry and looking forward to my Sunday lunch?

My early educational needs taught me about colours, words and sums, oh and the odd fairy tale with a moral message. The only way the hillside communicated with me in those early days was by the colours of the bluebells in spring and the mushrooms in the autumn. The trees were just trees and held no great purpose to me other than shade in the summer along with adventure and climbing skills, and the annual scrump of apples and berries would keep me regular when the sweet periods were lean. Looking back on those bits, at least I still have my own teeth along with being relatively healthy. An apple a day and all.

I like to think that the hillside saw me as a special person due to my frequent visits. Let's ask them, shall we?

Quercus was convinced the days of quarrying had finished, so he felt compelled to speak to the inhabitants of the hillside, well at least the ones that cared to listen. It appeared to all that the current pollution levels were a concern for all the trees and plants – they were happily growing well and prospering but they all felt that it could get more uncomfortable as the years progressed due to their carbon absorption being at around 90 per cent of their capacity. Corylus assured them all that if they were at full capacity within the next 20 years they would simply reject the excess pollution, and their need to produce more plants would cope with the surplus. Fraxinus also noted that the large stretch of motorway seen from the hillside gets busier year in year out, with most of the ancient willow either gone or hanging on for dear life, and he wondered whether this sight was a familiar one around the country.

A new member to the team was the Lawson cypress planted at the foot of the hillside. He greeted the others and said that from his early days in the London nurseries he had witnessed a sorry state of affairs on the planet. The trees and plants zoned in and listened with baited breath. It appeared that the motorway along with the automobile was starting to be a major thing around the cities of the UK, from dirty diesels to 4-star Rolls Royces. Not only had the roads expanded but also the towns and villages hugging the major road routes, as the post-war baby boomers were beginning to grow up and require space to live in. 'Trees and meadows in their path are ripped up and turned into car parks or large shopping malls,' said Lawson, and he went on to explain how the village had expanded. 'Try to imagine that multiplied by 100 or indeed a thousand in some cases,' he said. The hillside gasped and looked down upon the lowlands with a slight tear of sap. Quercus couldn't accept that their fate was the same as many ancient woodlands and meadows around the country, although deep down he held a strong fear. Corylus, always the voice of reason, explained that industry was leaving the village at an alarming rate, and without industry you have no growth in the world of humanity. The shy orchids of the damp slopes then voiced their concerns: their plight had been at the hand of human-kind, along with the ever hungry bracken. 'We as a collective have been reduced by half over the last 100 years due to agriculture and roads, and the hillside is our final stand for survival,' they said. The orchids asked Lawson if there were any similar survivors out there, and if so, could he give them any news of their whereabouts so they could extend their leaves out to them? Lawson's lack of reply said it all and confirmed their fears. Quercus assured the orchids that just because they hadn't been spotted didn't mean to say they were not there. Perhaps, like all the other rare orchids, they chose to seek refuge in a place not considered useful to humanity. 'You all keep strong,' he said. 'We are all rooting for you all.'

So as the roar of the jet plane thundered over them the trees fell silent, and as to whether they noticed me, for the moment the jury is still out.

Secondary education of sorts

From shorts to baggy cords and then tight drainpipe jeans, my age reached double figures. Comprehensive was looming for me and my twin sister, and suddenly, according to reports from my older brothers and sisters, I needed to man up and change my outlook on life. I'd only just about mastered the Ladybird books, only to be told I would be reading real books and working out proper sums, oh and *Grange Hill* is real. Bloody uniforms and blazers turned me from a snotty nosed kid ... well to a bigger snotty nosed kid. I didn't want all this – take me back to the soft teachers and the morning milk. Suddenly I was about to meet the kids of the other neighbouring tribes and don't forget your protractor and ballpoint pen. Pen and protractor? I'm still mastering the pencil and ruler. Talk about chucking me in at the deep end. Still, it didn't matter as I had the support of my older family ... Not! They were only too happy for me to make the same mistakes they had. Why should I get all the good luck promised to me by my primary teacher?

To be honest I hated it all: my first day in the asylum of mad kids, big bullies and bloody protractors. They broke us in gently with a school assembly in which I felt compelled to sit on the floor. They told us about the coming years, along with the great educational system we were about to become accustomed to. While my buddies Rob and Chris were nowhere to be seen, names were called, houses selected and rooms allocated. This was followed by us all being led away by our house teacher like poor wartime refugees, uncertain of our destination and future. We all looked at each other, not knowing names and with no introduction, judging each other only by our school uniform. My second-hand uniform resembled a throwback to the 60s while others trended the latest styles. They, unlike me, had caring parents who watched out not only for their future but for their image amongst the crowd of newcomers. That's probably a bit unfair to my parents but I really lacked any guidance from them due to my poor upbringings. I liked to think that when I started comp the learning levels would be reset for all, due to the different subjects taught like science and home economics. Not so, I can assure you.

My skills were nurtured by myself without any guidance from teachers – some could say a natural in the arts plus on the work benches of wood and metal. Maths and English were not my strong points (no comment) but I really enjoyed history and science. I just wish now that I'd studied more, but my friendship with others meant more to me than the educational system. My friends hankered after a post-punk era in the early 80s, and stereotypically my poor upbringing pigeon-holed my position at school: not a bully, not really noticed; just a kid who hung out with all the wrong 'uns in class. This band of brothers' loyalty would soon set up my future steps into the big world. To be honest I really wanted to learn, but it would have looked a bit nerdy amongst my mates. So as the deal with Rob turned from him giving me an apple core to me giving him a bread roll or Mars bar due to his need to spend his school dinner money on fags, we slowly began to grow up. Lower school discos would also segregate our musical likes into two tribes of punks and mods with the odd scuffle between records. To be totally honest now, I liked the sound of the Jam along with a deep secret of liking Abba (shhh, keep that one to yourself), so I was just keeping up appearances to fit in. Don't get me wrong, I liked Stiff Little Fingers and the Damned, more for their lyrical content of anti-government and anti-society but hey, are they just protest songs like in the 60s and perhaps a bit of the 50s, all dressed up in zips and belts? Freedom of speech in the twentieth century made great divisions but also made people wake up to their surroundings in a *Citizen Smith* way.

Sorry, you may be wondering what all this has to do with the hillside plants and indeed the universe, but there is a reason for my non-horticultural blurb, which is to introduce the awakening of my own futile existence on this planet. We all fit into moulds and can so easily lose our way in life

– my teenage years changed from climbing trees and rolling in the grass to BMX bikes, girls and underachievement all within a space of four years. I stopped dreaming and began to start worrying and trying to impress. I really didn't know what I wanted. Running was one of the few things I was quite good at, and I just wanted to break school records in cross country and bunny hop the highest pole on my BMX bike.

Playing soldier

My awakening strangely came in the form of a military hobby that was the army cadets. Most of my friends were in it, and although I initially wasn't allowed due to being underage, when I was old enough I joined up – by choice, may I add. Previous villagers over the centuries had been press ganged and made to join up whether they liked it or not, war then being part of the weekly discussion on humanity's lips. My need to join up was to experience the gun in the firing range, plus join up with my mates on the weekend manoeuvres, oh and to play at being a soldier, due to my armies of toy metal tanks and plastic soldiers at home. What they didn't tell me was that I had to wear itchy shirts and jumpers and polish my boots every day and take orders from a spotty-faced young Hitler. The British Army uniform of the 60s was a hand-me-down to us all, unless your parents bought you some lightweights from the Army Surplus store, and it was all very uncomfortable to wear in an untailored, baggy and itchy way. Its purpose was to blend in to the countryside, and I can relate to that, as our past mud fights on the building sites had taught us to duck and hide along with developing a great sense of camouflage and the element of surprise. So a trained cadet I was, following the nasty initiation ceremony of wedging which made me one of the light infantry troops of the village. Just give me a gun to shoot!

All this was to prepare me for the return to the hillside, where we would learn the techniques of blending in to the habitat, a little bit like *Dad's Army* but for kids, no one really knowing what to do with a bivvy bag and a ball of string. My introduction to the ferns would be a bloody one as I pulled up the bracken with my bare hands, underestimating its sharpness. With my hands all bleeding I just had to carry on and fight. We would march up the hillside in single file, all cammi-pasted up and itchy, to play our war games in the field next to the large Georgian house. We had to take cover and be prepared for the odd crow scarer or firework. It didn't matter because we had a drill purpose rifle to play with and pretend to fire upon an imaginary enemy.

Now the hillside had begun to take notice of me and my band of toy soldiers. Quercus looked down with great intrigue along with all his family. War had never been so tame: no injuries or loss of life, just play fighting. Beneath the lower wood we camped out to get one of our stars on our epaulette. For me this was great fun, and knowing the wood like the back of my hand made me the perfect scout between divisions. My cross country training gave me plenty of stamina to run up and down the ancient hill fort like a fast whippet. Some joked, others took the piss, but I on the other hand was just pleased to run amongst the trees and hide within the undergrowth. One time I stumbled onto the floor and looked up into the wonder of the trees' canopy. It was early morning and the sun was just starting to rise. I remember seeing the glisten of the wet leaves from the sun's rays – quite magical. Quercus was there along with Fraxinus and Corylus, and they turned their solar harvesters to capture the moment for me. In that split second a carefully planned manoeuvre was being performed for me by the trees of the hillside. Lucky moment I guess?

Sometime before my arrival that early morning the hillside teams were being assembled to do their morning battle cry. They like all plants felt the planet's turn due to their anchoring on the planet, and they all sensed the sun rising; its warmth slowly but surely coming towards them. Fraxinus and co decided to dedicate that morning's show to the next human who visited the hillside, their hope being that that person would get to experience their display. The morning was perfect; no clouds, just enough water content in the air, and to date no human had really taken it all in until this fine morn when I fell to the floor and looked skyward. The last successful encounter like this had been by the foreign traveller who'd camped out under Fraxinus all those centuries back. His legacy was the carpet of cyclamen under Fraxinus's trunk, grown from the seeds he'd unknowingly transported, not forgetting the celandine and primrose as well. Humanity from that point on had had no time to sit and stare – just too much in a hurry.

Fraxinus and co were pleased that it was me that witnessed their light display, due to my many walks up the hillside with Pupsy, as the timing had never been right before, in my rush to walk the dog and get home. The weekend of military manoeuvres on the hillside gave the trees an ideal slot in which to impress me; naturally though in a few days or so I forgot the whole experience due to my school commitments. Funny how the one thing I wanted to learn at school was never really on the curriculum, with my only initial introduction to plants having taken place in my primary years. Sad, methinks. My dad, bless him, tried to teach me the way of the grub along with the pruning of a rose but failed to make any impact on my attention. My paper round gave me all the pocket money I needed without the need for a labouring day in the garden where the hourly rate was poor to nothing. If someone had picked me up and taught me the ways of the plants then, well I could have been the next Geoff Hamilton? For me the understanding of the leaf vein compared to our vein, the food stored to the food made, along with the plant's need to grow and spread out would have put me on an early road to discovery. Thankfully I had the memory of the trees embedded in my head so that I can write this story around it, instead of being a plastic punk rocker with the craving to put flowers in my hair.

More wars and disputes

Mini wars broke out around the globe in the late 70s and early 80s just to keep things ticking over for the warring tribes. The Falklands was a battle too far away for me to worry about but Thatcher had other ideas about our lonely rock in the South Atlantic. Other conflicts were fought by the Arabs and the Christians in the Middle East. Their military had caught up with the West so they were armed with Kalashnikovs and tanks under the rule of dictators. So the Second World War just kept on rolling on throughout the planet.

As the world began to burn on the planet's surface, the oil-rich Arab states became the next developing nations, and amongst the sand and palm trees they created their own oasis of popularity amongst the oil giants. They dictated to the West the price of a barrel, which made us all begin to feel the pinch when filling up our combustion engines, and taxes were kept high by the governments just to fuel their own ambitions within the world of economic supremacy. Oh, and the ozone layer was getting that little bit thinner due to the 80s' need for hairspray and deodorant – a good excuse not to blame the petrol companies then for the rising CO_2 levels around the globe? Bring back the 60s, when they were all just a bunch of sweaty free-loving kinda people.

School leaver to worker

School came and went quicker than I wanted, but I was relieved to get off that train of madness. I passed all the subjects put in front of me – not high scores, just enough to scrape through as a bordering underachiever in a system that failed me. So when my head of house got me in his office and talked about my prospective future, his words were similar to the ones he'd said to all the limited range pupils; things like 'I can't see you going on to sixth form, so you'd do just as well to leave now.' Thanks for the chance, Mr Gimber. Naturally, as you do, I promptly flooded the upstairs toilets on my departure, adding to the decades of water stains on the classroom ceiling: underachievers unite with the Vs up to you. Oh, and to make matters worse I was homeless at the age of 15 due to our eviction from our council house. How did that happen, you may ask. Well apparently lack of rent payments by my mum. I don't wish to go into all the details. I would much prefer to put all that behind me; the hard knock life just got harder for me, that's all. Post eviction, the family got completely split up to various locations, and me, my twin sister and my older brother were forced to grow up long before our time. We never experienced the luxury of saving up some money to buy the things we wanted in our late teens. Instead we were forced to go to work in whatever job best suited ourselves and pay for rent and food. The small fact that I wanted to join the army was passed aside. It had all been going so well for me and then bang, my life's turned upside down. All my friends were supportive but they were trying to just grow up themselves. Naturally my early adulthood ripped me away from all that I held dear, from my cosy bedroom to the weekly walks up the hill – me and my sister were forced to leave our native village and move from town to town like refugees. We endured a mouldy caravan, then experienced the luxury of plumbing in a short term let above a local vet's, and finally settled in a council flat by the seaside. Sounds idyllic? Not so. I just wanted to get a break from all the madness and live the life of a true adolescent. Still, at least we had a roof over our heads with the combined support of each other to complain about whose turn it was to go to the launderette or do the shopping.

My mates told me how great the 80s were but for me I just want to forget it. The hillside community just waited for my return, as they, like all the plants and trees, were used to the changes of routine by humanity. On a planetary scale, the world was changing at an alarming rate due to the need for coffee, grain and burgers, with the local lords fattening up the pheasants for the shoot only to be wasted by the hunter. This not for need but for want attitude changed humanity's outlook on the way we grew our food. Do we need the extra piece of cake after the large Sunday roast? Perhaps one more cup of coffee will give me a bit more vigour? There were half-eaten loaves of bread in the fridge because the burger and fries seemed more appealing. Before the demand for food and substance was so high, North America was already at a tipping point in production, and the south Americas would soon be the next table provider. Brazil was like any other third world civilisation around the globe which would capitalise on western gluttony, so as they dismantled the rainforest bit by bit to make way for the cow and the bean, slowly they were reducing the lung capacity of the planet. What started as a slight splutter would result in an unhealthy cough around the globe, especially when the seas warmed and the tornados turned. The scientists like many before them warned the corporates of their actions, but it all fell on deaf ears, as the size and scale of the forest made their warnings easy to dismiss.

The trees around the world began to notice the effects of all this damaging behaviour by humankind, so when the weather charts began to rise and the water began to dry up the famines of the African nations were the first to hit the headlines, thanks to the caring pop stars. Suddenly we had a group of people willing to make a difference with the odd song or two to help feed the world, while others sang their protest songs for the rainforests, along with more local Irish issues. Who would have thought the musicians of the world would take the time to care about something that was hundreds of miles away? But yes, under that thick head of hair and some lively shirts and suits was a bunch of protest singers trying to get out.

Did all this affect our local hillside? Well not really, or did it? Let's listen to what they were saying.

Tucked away on the hillside were the little cottages and farms built up by centuries of local workers wishing to have a quiet way of life. Their colour TVs and radios would remind them of all the world's troubles, and while they would be intrigued by the planet's problems from the safety of their armchairs, the minute they walked out the door all was forgotten. Quercus and co were already there, night and day, and would pick up any slight change in the air. They'd already talked about the air pollution, the summers though seemed to get more intense with a slight overlap into the winter. A series of mild winters would soon follow, leading to the increase of fungi and pathogens in the air, and the insects would thrive under the warm greenhouse of the planet's dome. This would lead to an increase in chemicals used by humankind, not only in the fields but also amongst the rose-filled gardens and polytunnels, and suddenly the annual crop spray would be mimicked by the keen gardeners, led like farmers by the chemical industries. So as Quercus and co assessed the damage of the increased threat amongst the wood folk they realised that this was part of nature's way, in the way that the leaf miner caterpillar nibbles undercover, but the tree's leaf is still able to absorb all its nutrients, albeit a bit restricted by this little insect. The other insects of the wood would either tolerate him or if lucky eat him, so as to continue the cycle of life amongst the wood. Humanity sought a solution but was beaten by this clever insect leading them to tolerate the blotchy leaf in their great parks. Humankind had always had a stifled respect for the trees, especially as the scientists were telling them that trees were the lungs of the planet while human life continued to smoke and choke. This prompted a nationwide body of tree experts slamming tree preservation orders onto our ancients. Humanity had never been so policed before.

Now, if a person wished to cut an old tree down in their garden they would have to consult the local council first, although some took matters into their own hands, which left the neighbours twitching and the fines flowing. Some trees not native to the area had a reduced appeal to the tree wardens but earned equal respect, particularly when they homed the odd woodpecker or owl. All this began to change the rights of the plants and trees, especially when the boundaries were tight and the Leylandii grew fast – leading to discontent in the cramped gardens and households within the towns and cities of the country. Some plants brought in by the plant hunters of the Victorian era began to be shunned by the local populace due to their invasive takeover of the woodlands and parks, while others stayed and enjoyed the fuss by the non-believers in native flowers, all because the growers told them they were so much better. Past mistakes by the hunters and growers were ignored by the gardeners when told by the experts on the TV or in glossy mags, 'Lift and store your dahlias, protect your frost tender plants, oh, and keep the natives at bay with the odd spray of napalm.' Your garden would surely be tamed and controlled by you because this was your little Eden of tranquillity on the planet. Remember to prick out your petunias and spray your roses, turn the ground on a double dig rotation and clear away your leaves from your soil – you can always add chemicals in the spring to help boost vigour and growth. Try to ignore what the past gardeners have taught you when working your garden because we want to sell you more plants and products on an annual basis so as to sustain our growth and rule the world of horticultural excellence.

Not wishing to get bitter about the increase of the ignorant gardener, all the actions were to result in a chain reaction of bad decisions around the globe. You might say, 'What can Mr Gardener be doing wrong on his local patch down the allotment?' He's just a post-war grower who'd relied on the old skills, only to be converted to the lazy ways of control and gadgets. To be fair, the TV gardeners in the 80s were teaching us the old school principles of how to grow and develop a successful garden, but like many were guided by ratings and, behind the scenes, manufacturers of products. Not the Beeb way, may I say?

Landscape gardener

As we rip through the 80s and into the 90s with all the pizzazz of the American influences like Hollywood and fast food, our bright coloured jumpers and sticky hair were replaced by chinos and leather jackets; a more casual fashion had emerged. Our hair got shorter but the need to prosper was dawning on us all – get a mortgage, tie down a good job, probably get married? None of the above for me as I was still just trying to pay the rent and keep a steady job going. But was my path to be similar to that of my parents and indeed all my brothers and sisters? With their succession of marriages, kids and divorces to follow I was clever enough to avoid those mistakes early on. Is there anything in the rule book of life that says you have to do all those things? One thing is certain though – death and taxes will catch up with us all, but I'm still waiting for my final demand. From teenagers to adults we were transformed in a blink of an eye, and having no one to look up to and no respect for myself meant I was going through the motions. Level 42's song 'Running in the Family' had never been so right.

As usual I digress again from my path and the message of this story, but the centuries of learning and lessons taught me as a human were fitting in quite well with my place not only on the planet but within the universe. Like everyone from the cavemen to the Norman invaders I was just following the beat of the drum dictated by society and government. I really needed a change of direction. Thanks to the offer of a job from my brother, who was working in landscape gardening for a large commercial contractor, I embarked on the same career (not on a par with Lancelot Capability Brown). My new title of landscape gardener exceeded my goal in life. I felt similar to a bin man or road sweeper, with a better sounding job title but the same hourly rate. Being self-employed back in the late 80s was a turbulent time of work or no work from week to week. The developers of the supermarkets and business parks were controlled by the world markets, which controlled our chance of work that week or month. Suddenly though, due to an economic boom, we were busy landscaping massive business parks and malls. These were all lavishly planted up with shrubs and trees all in geometric blocks and lines, from litter bins to colourful flowers, and the landscape architects of the time saw their chance to be the next Capability Brown amongst the many thousands of competitors. Others took to the stage within the gardening shows around the country to peddle their wares and ideas – the rising media appeal could turn the simplest gardener into a household name amongst the potting sheds and stately homes of the country. Us, well we just followed the plan and mulched the borders. All the glory was given to the person who designed the land at the glitzy opening ceremonies. We the workers were confined to the outdoors with our faces up against the glass: show me the bar, mate, I'm buying tonight. If I am truly honest I really didn't see what all the fuss was about; I just concentrated on my wage packet and my overtime, caught in the middle of a vicious circle of laundry and bills. But good honest graft along with the neatness we commanded on our sites gave us a relatively good reputation amongst our peers. There were no medals or congrats at this point … well at least if you don't aim for them you can't be disappointed. I put this down to lack of praise from my parents. From those early days out in the fields of landscaping I learnt my plant knowledge by planting thousands of each particular variety, force fed I suppose. It didn't matter though, because I was beginning to get it, not only the Latin names but the complex plans in front of us. We had to plant blocks of shrubs in threes and fives, learning their potential for growth and their habits, within our 12-monthly maintenance regime.

Now at this point we had students from local colleges with us to learn about landscaping on a work experience scheme. They were taught about the science first, the practical later, and a lazy bunch of gardeners they turned out to be! Still, they went on to guide others and design other such business parks around the country, and these students gave me a small insight into their world, especially when they had to learn the weeds before the plants. How weird, I thought. We are only told how to kill 'em or avoid them, not learn about them, but looking back their way was the best way to learn about plants. But yet again I still couldn't break free from that comprehensive school bracket of being a non-learner amongst a gang of uneducated, hard-working blokes that were a result of education's failures. The students, like the ivy and the bramble of the meadow, were tolerated but regularly put in their place by those of us with practical experience. I was destined to stay put, however, whereas these brambles and ivies had high hopes of reaching the top of the tree in their fields.

The plants and indeed all the wild herbs had yet to reach out and talk to me, as seeing the dandelion in the lawn or in the cracks of the pavement only served to be a nuisance to my neat approach. Anything other than the non-native collection of shrubs was hoed out, sprayed out and kicked out of the ground – slash and burn was my philosophy amongst all the other teams of grounds maintenance guys. Machinery made the day a lot easier and the chemicals would reduce the amount of work by another three quarters, but I was just following suit in a world of similar practices. So if anybody was to tell me then that the bees and butterflies were in decline and the polar ice caps were melting, I would have probably said, 'Warmer summers, then, with less bugs to worry about'. As I write this I really feel guilty about my past, but like all things that are learnt in life you can easily try to reverse the problem rather than ignoring it all completely. The planet at this point was in a state of flux. With the nuclear age came the bomb along with the power stations – Chernobyl in Ukraine was a lesson learnt post the Second World War, but we still built power stations like it, with the reassurance that they are safer than flying a plane through a lightning strike within the eye of a storm with just one prop. Well that's alright then, we can put our trust in you; just keep the lights on please. If only I'd had the wisdom and guidance of Corylus to put me on the path to discovery …

Recession and unemployment

Thatcher's boom boys had spent all their plastic and over-extended their credit and friends, resulting in a broken country once again. My crikey, it only seemed a decade since the last crisis of unemployment had hit our shores. Too old for a YTS, with not enough time to start a new career or apprenticeship meant all the more reason for me to pay my way, but I ended up being unemployed, on the dole and just a statistic amongst the millions. Still, I had drive and enthusiasm, and hitting the skids changed my life's journey, on which me and my partner took up an art class to pass the time until something better came along. Fancy that, me being a student, minus the attitude, greasy hair, baggy jeans and baked bean diet (visions of *The Young Ones* spring to mind). My achievement at school of O Level art was enough credence for me to consider a career in the arts, Luvvy, but to be honest I couldn't handle the nudes and the abstract stuff. I just preferred to sketch everything, before being told I was doing it all wrong. Schooling had let me down again I guess? Realising there could be no future in this due to the past masters only being wealthy after their death, it all seemed utterly pointless, so we both promptly started to kick the tin can around the streets of Weston-super-Mare, taking up free pastimes like walking and reading along with economising our dole to the bare bones. Perhaps this was our war moment in peacetime Britain – a little bit of suffering and rationing never did our ancestors any harm, did it? Fast food and high living can be a detriment to your mind, body and soul, and having the odd lean period in our lives makes us more grounded, planet people. The plants around the planet require only enough substance to grow and breathe, and once this is achieved they can produce their own food in a self-sufficient way, like the starving masses in the war-torn areas of Africa during the 80s – all they required was the grain to grow crops in order to survive. Sadly, they were deprived of the simplest of survival needs due to the ravages of war, when their only wish was to return to their farms and live their lives without any handout or fuss. My life at that time only required the same as those poor farmers, given that we had nothing to show off to the world, with no waste, no baggage – only our hearts and minds.

The hillside had had its fill of waste after a decade of being used as a land-fill. A typical solution to the world's waste: find a hole and chuck a load of rubbish in it. This was similar to my dad's ways of burying an old spring mattress in the garden. He couldn't quite work out once it was placed in the ground why the soil wouldn't go back in? Puzzling, I thought, but the solution was simple, Father. Where did you think the soil was going to go? Volume versus mass and all that science. Still, we had a great crop of spring onions the following year, guffaw guffaw. Abandoned quarries around the country suffered the same fate as the hillside, along with the smell and the vermin. Once the dozer has compacted enough plastic and paper, top it up with a little soil so it doesn't all blow away, oh and remember to allow the methane to evaporate before you do anything with it. My eviction from the village spared me the years of the acrid smell of waste on the north-easterly wind; the locals nonetheless got used to it due to being accustomed to country living with the seasonal muck spread. For me, the quarry and indeed the tip seemed a complete waste of time (pardon the pun) given the metal extracted compared to the amount of ecological and archaeological damage caused. Perhaps in time we might even consider recycling and reusing like all good gardeners do on a weekly basis. My understanding of recycling was based on an early experience when my neighbour Lindsay required all the tin foil we could muster so that she could have valuable cancer treatment, along with the stacks of tied up paper for the Boy Scouts on our streets, but now I get it. Plastics would soon dominate the world through convenient packaging and cheap toys from Asia, but no one told me to keep the box of my action man as it may be worth a bit in years to come. Instead we, like all of the European nations, were being slowly swamped with the cheapest counterfeits from the Asian countries. These developing nations, like the south Americas, would change the planet's delicate balance all in the name of progress for beef and a Barbie doll.

Realisation

It didn't take too long for me to realise the workings of the world, but like most of the little people of the world our voice is small, like the orchids and wild flowers in the meadow on the hillside. My precipice was when I'd had enough of being laid off by countless companies, even though the hazard of being self-employed was that you were truly dispensable. Match that with the lack of care and money in the commercial landscaping scene, all bundled up in a bish bosh tight budget schedule. Going it alone was at first my only option but now I realise it was one of my better decisions in my career. However, friends and family all had their steady jobs and secured mortgages, while I like the plants was still struggling to root. Well if all else failed I only had myself to blame when the rent wasn't paid or the cupboard was bare. I had my student experience, my rock bottom dole hand out, oh and a few days on the bins to make me realise that I had a career in gardening ahead of me. Yes, a simple gardener – not landscaper, not horticulturist, a gardener. My dad would be proud. I started out small on a lot of small gardens with a competitive cheap hourly rate around my home town. Not much different to the jobbing gardeners or ex-factory workers laid off by their industry, all chasing their tail from day to day to make a reasonable daily wage. The jobbers had their redundancy and pension to fall back on, I on the other hand worked from hand to mouth. I could have so easily given up the chase for work and gone on the sick for a suspected bad back with all the gifts of mobility and crisis loans, but no, I was a proud man, not wishing to scrounge off the state. I'd stand up and walk tall.

Quercus and co would have been proud of me if they were to hear of my life's struggle. Sadly though, our untimely eviction from the village had pulled me away from their gaze and thoughts, and I jealously thought that I might have been replaced by some other wandering walker in the woods on the hillside. Still, the elastic band pulling me back home was starting to get tighter and tighter. I just didn't realise it.

Fate

Do you believe in fate, dear reader? I do, along with karma and all that, but at this point I was starting to be led wayward towards the bright lights of fame and fortune … No, just fame. I had grand designs of being the next best thing plucked from obscurity and placed in front of a TV camera.

The London horticulturists were to blame for my need to succeed in a world full of underachievers and glory seekers. Garden design was the new craze on the telly along with 60-second makeovers and property pro-grammes. *Ground Force* and *Changing Rooms* were topping the bill, com-plete with their mdf and bish bosh rushed creations. You might say a typ-ical example of how not to do it, but hey, it makes great viewing figures. What's next, celebrity dole seekers or untalented Barbies and Kens? The mind boggles. Everybody was talking about it; everybody wanted to join the plastic revolution of Hollywood-style garden and temporary make-overs. Like them I was tempted and eventually snared into the trap of a life of false promises and dreams. It's at this point that I will direct you to my first book, *The Woodcutter's Story*, to save me having to write it all over again – a story within a story, shall we say. To cut a long story short, just in case you don't read the other story, it's all based on my life creating RHS show gardens, but portrayed through characters named after native trees (so as to protect the innocent). It has highs and lows with a happy ending. Well, as happy as could be expected anyway. I will leave it up to you to make your own mind up.

Cash spent and in debt up to my ears, consecutive self-funded projects and show gardens had been perhaps a venture too far. Lesson learnt. One thing was for sure, I kept true to my old school principles of putting it down to bad experience and getting on with things in life – not crying into my beer, not asking for any sympathy or handouts, just pure determination to keep moving forward and when the bar is slightly raised try my damned-est to get over it, even if it takes a few tries.

Doing all the show garden stuff did teach me a thing or two about plants and gardens, along with my diploma in garden design. What? I hear you say. Yes, the boy done good and got a letterhead credential. The need to earn a diploma put me a little above the Boy Scouts in my field of work, and those teachings were enough for me to write this story based on my course essay on the history of garden design. Like I said, some things happen for a reason, and the diploma along with my artistic tendencies made me able to not only write about garden design but also to draw garden designs. None of that CAD or 3D stuff, just simple pencil and paper drawings giving my niche client a piece of art to enjoy in their dusty sideboard drawer. I was now known as a garden designer because my letterhead told me so, but the hardest thing was to convince a non-believer that my design was the best thing since Andre Le Notre or Capability Brown. Who are they, I hear them ask … heavens. Everybody wants a deck, a patio or a pergola because it's been seen on the TV. The great shows promote the best concrete products and the next best plant to buy, along with all the egos of the top designers, but do they really think that Mrs Jones wants to spend a quarter of a million on an 8x10 plot … Well no. Get real!

Most people post-recession and crash were trying to keep their homes, with the brave trying to crawl up the property ladder on minuscule budgets that weren't really enough to pay for a patio. This is where I came in to help the struggling few at probably a detriment to myself financially. You see, all I wanted to do was plant up gardens, not concrete them over; I wanted the struggling home owner to see the potential of a beautiful garden as a selling point. Lobbing a deck in the corner with the odd token pot is not my idea of a garden – you can save that for the pub garden or the shopping precinct. So what do they ask from me? Miracles on a small budget. Yes, after all, gardening is only a low-paid job, right? Well no, it's up there with the plumbers and electricians in my eyes. Don't worry though, we've just bought a new kitchen with the extended mortgage due to a slight price rise in the market, so we may just have another couple of hundred to spend for you to work your magic, Mark …? Not to mention the new car out the front, which is on the tick because we thought we needed to treat ourselves. As you can imagine I'm walking out of the back gate at this point – they don't need me, they need a financial advisor to counsel them in the best way forward on their spending. You could say that this scenario was happening all around the country at this point, with everyone brainwashed by the instant two-day garden by the experts in their field. If I had sat down with the nation and told them it isn't possible to create a beautiful space over two days, and in fact the perfect garden would probably take you years to achieve, I would have been laughed out of the door. Don't get me wrong, I'm all for people doing well for themselves. But as they move out of their small shoe box into a slightly larger one they only tend to inherit the same dismal garden, and when the developers build on the flood plains the buyers inherit a bog or marsh. My confusion and disbelief is apparent now because no one really thinks things through properly, and along with all the past problems of the planet the natural landscape is the one to suffer through lack of planning.

This brings me back to the hillside. Peace at last. Calm yourself, Mark, please.

The trees saw from the hillside the amount of progress by humankind, with the dust rising from the quarries to the east and the ever-expanding once quaint garden centre, now that the rise of the machines had made the car park larger and the polytunnels smaller. The garden centre owners' need to grow plants on site had now changed to favour cheaper mass production elsewhere in Europe or the UK; suddenly it was all about retail more than horticulture. The village at this point had expanded well beyond its original boundaries.

The trees on the hillside asked themselves where have all these people come from and why do they choose to settle in a village with little agriculture and non-existent factories? Corylus getting the word from the street said they are all a product of a post-war baby boom, and no current wars have served to cull their progress. Fraxinus added to the relaxed chat, 'What does that mean for the rest of the meadow folk and the willows on the flood plains? Are they to be lost forever?'

'Not necessarily,' Quercus added, 'there just needs to be a shift in their patterns towards all of nature. We are safe,' he added, 'because of the hill fort and the new laws of tree protection. Someday the meadows will get the same respect that we have seen in previous centuries from humankind. I do feel sorry for them, though,' he also added. 'It's because of their strained seed that their kind is becoming weaker. We absorb the carbons so that they can breathe relatively safely but our fill is nearly up. Little children in the meantime are choking in the cities due to the pollution, their little lungs not strong enough to cope with the gases around them. Water courses are polluted, and there is the ever-present threat of hosepipe bans, which unlike us denies them a source that is part of life itself – we store and drain what we need, but they take and overindulge. They can't help the way it is, purely because that's how their life has been built: on a throwaway society with a take it now attitude and sod the future.'

Corylus thought that was a bit harsh of Quercus. It seemed his old age had made him a bit cantankerous and bitter towards humanity, and Quercus promptly apologised and kept schtum. 'Listen everybody,' Corylus said, 'I feel there is change afoot amongst humankind, starting here on our doorstep. Can you remember that young lad tripping over and falling to the ground only to look up and witness our display of light and leaf?' They all nodded. 'Well he may just be coming back to the hillside in the form of a much older chap full of life's experiences. He will give us hope, along with the kind family which brings him here. Patience, everyone, patience.'

Not wishing to guess at plants having foresight or a crystal ball of the future, let's just say that they have a knack of predicting weather patterns and changes in nature. The plants and trees have been connected to this large lump of molten rock for billions of years, and they unlike us can pick up the smallest seismic movement along with the warming and cooling of the planet long before we get to feel it. Our seasons are dictated by our journey around our sun – that's all that we can relate to, and when things go off plan we question what's going on through multiple computations and charts. The plants and trees like the biggest super computer have all things on planet Earth worked out. Well that's my theory anyway.

No one really seemed to play on the hillside anymore. It got, well, a bit serious with the 90s heralding a new toy and machines that would keep humanity locked into their homes for hours on end. Everybody got mobile but stayed at home, they all enjoyed the world without the need to explore it, and suddenly the technology started to make Georgy Porgy a common sight, not only in the adults but in the kids as well. Agoraphobia and SAD were also on the rise due to the mixed up state of minds of some, and seemed to be untreatable and incurable. Suddenly the 'get out and get on with things' attitude was forgotten and replaced with sympathy. Humankind started to mollycoddle their young from an early age, given that the world was portrayed as a dangerous place by the media. A lonely old man walking in the wood was considered a bit weird and out of place, and potentially threatening. To look or stare at someone would also appear to offend, when all they were probably doing was daydreaming due to a sleepless night on the sofa. The hillside noticed this as the walkers began to dwindle due to people's paranoia of who else might be there. Having a vicious dog on the street was also a big symbol of who you were in society. Confusion was added when a polite couple walked both a poodle and a Rottweiler together through a park full of Staffies and pit bulls, whose leads and collars only indicated their intent towards other dogs.

The hillside had had its glory years of the modest gardeners in the small cottages that hugged the slopes of the wood, but people had grown old and died, some passing their properties down to their next of kin, others putting them up for auction to pay for their care. As new occupants moved in, previously treasured cottage gardens and allotments were neglected and swallowed up by the meadow teams who had patiently waited for the land to revert back to its roots. In some places the bramble and nettle would dominate, in other places the buttercup and fescue were equally appreciative of the fertile, well-dug soil. Some gardens would have the opportunity of a 60-second makeover by the neighbouring garden designer, and driven by the trends of the Chelsea set they would ignore the way of the wood and expect and demand the foreign plants to succeed, adorning their gardens with topiary and large shrubs all in the name of low maintenance, height and structure – they would collectively mould the gardens into a picture of simplicity. The meadow teams with a combined woodland edge contingent moved in and out as the tenants of the houses came and went, only to be pushed to one side each time by the digger or spade, leaving the plants to rise and regroup when the opportunity arose again. Sadly their progress was always halted by the intense neatness of the gardening teams: mow and cut, shape and plant, with little or no clue of what they were doing, just as long as they got paid. The woodland advance along the meadow edges would also force the likes of nettle and bramble to grow diagonally so as to capture the sun's rays. They almost appeared to shun their woodland friends but had no other choice due to the constant cutting of the verge by the local gardeners. They were both between a rock and a hard place, with little chance of advance or retreat. Nettle, along with bramble, was gracious in defeat so they tactically decided to go sideways to avoid any confrontation between the two frontiers. Oh how the mighty fall!

An episode of pure destruction was suffered by the cyclamen, cowslip and celandine under the base of one of Fraxinus's siblings when a disgruntled gardener strimmed and slashed their growth to the ground then applied the napalm from above, all under strict orders by the owners to keep the weeds down. Some survived to tell the tale, others just burned in the ground in a slow but agonising death. The cyclamen's seed had fortunately made it to the outer fringes under a newly planted laurel, courtesy of the ants last summer, with the celandine and cowslip fighting on bravely to the bitter end. Trees like the field maple around the garden perimeter had to put up with the build-up of soil around their trunks, only to slowly rot their cambium life blood, leaving them half formed in a mangled scarecrow way. The insects couldn't put up with the constant fuss by the new occupiers so promptly left their home of thousands of years to seek salvation in the other derelict barns and homes neglected by humanity. Driveways were built along with walls to divide people's homes from the primitive wood. Dahlias and heathers planted in the dry or shady ground acted first as fine caviar for the meadow slugs and snails to feast on, but then failed due to the wrong soil type and aspect, leaving the ivy and elder to take over and poach the plants' neat little square of compost, leaving only a plant label to indicate their previous existence.

What a waste, I hear you say, and yes it was. If only the humans were to let go and see what the wind blew in, stop and think what they were doing and what they really wanted to achieve from this endless bottomless pit of money spent. So much potential was hidden in the garden, but a bit of patience was the only solution to allow the return of the native species in a garden full of non-native plants. Some got it right over the years by planting the correct trees and plants – probably more by luck than judgement. Laurels were planted to screen a wall, along with native hedgerows and spurge, all in a kind of hit and miss tribute to the ancient ways of the hillside. The insects ebbed and flowed in their hunt for food. They naturally found a constant supply of food within the neighbouring wood, but felt the need to spread their wings amongst the meadow in a futile waste of time search for nectar. Some plants would return amongst the nettle and bramble only to be chewed back tight by the sheep or mower, and with no places left to rest they simply died in their field. And when the NPKs were applied on the lawn to boost the colour and vigour, everything that was trying to grow found it a bit too rich to survive in. The moss and native plants were killed, whilst the grasses were able to grow better on a thin layer of top soil. The areas that had once been meadow were turned into manicured lawns that were no longer compatible for the survival of the natives.

This little episode of chemical warfare left the meadow teams really upset, as they had grown up with each other for many centuries. Their tapestry of life was slowly being unthreaded in front of them. The fescue felt guilty that her seed was allowed to flourish over her family and friends in the meadow. But she just had to keep on going and hope that one day they would return to their full glory. Slowly, though, she saw the disappearance of the orchids and the rattle, and at one point she wondered about her own future due to the ever-expanding homes and roads around her. Relief came when Corylus reassured her that the other plants were still around her but not close to her, and this gave her great strength. It turns out they were having a whale of a time in the adjacent field, due to a little-known cattle disease that wiped out the farmer's livelihood. The planet gave and took away life sometimes, just to reset the equilibrium slightly.

Springtime again awakened the trees on the hillside, after they'd spent a long winter hunkered down in their roots enjoying the rest after last year's fruitful display. So as the sun slowly edged higher over the southern horizon, their buds started to emerge, some sooner than others. Quercus was first to get up from his slumber and then somewhat reluctantly Fraxinus and Corylus followed. Words like 'the early bird' and all don't cut any mustard when you're bedding down nicely in a covering of thick leaf mould. As the saying goes, 'Oak before ash, we'll have a splash. Ash before oak, we're in for a soak.' So they all prepared themselves for a dry summer and dug deep. Eventually they were all beginning to work in tandem on their first leaf unfurl towards the sun to the east, then they slowly adjusted their pitch as it moved westward. Like all the plants of the world they worshiped their sun god, only to reset themselves the following morn. The light gave them life, with the moon providing a reflective beam for them to dream on in the evenings. They are there when we are born to provide us with clean air, then once we have passed they simply continue their giving for future mammals to survive. Humanity just took it all for granted as they continued to strip the lands of all their giving properties, but they then began to wonder why the land was flooding more – don't we have drains and ditches? Why is the air quality poor in our cities – can't the wind blow it all away? The ice caps are melting due to global warming, well I will stock up on sun cream then! All these problems we inherit from our ancestors as we seek perfection and wealth.

Now I thought that all older folk were at one with nature, gardens and grow your own due to their parents' influence in the war years, but I was wrong. Instead the powers that be shoved them all into tower blocks or care homes where little or no garden was available to them on a daily basis. The wealthy elderly folk had their gardeners who would mow and trim according to what grew the fastest, or throw in a bed of annuals in the spring if they required a splash of colour. Perhaps the odd hanging basket here and there to show off their brilliantly white wall, which encased a home full of bleach bottles and dusters. Oh, we don't want to fuss over the garden; we have far too much to do on our laptops and in our coffee chats. Let's concrete the drive over, put the lawn to gravel and keep it ... well, all low maintenance. Evict the slow worms from under the shed, burn out the hedgehog in the pampas grass, oh and no nibbles for the birds. They can go next door where the garden is a right mess, full of brambles with a smelly stagnant pond next to a shed that I'm sure is home to rats or foxes? 'It's our home, we will do what we want with it' was the attitude, so the generations of wildlife would have to move out into the sticks and await the next bull-dozer to arrive to drive them on into the sea.

The shambolic tapestry of life holds no meaning to the houses built on the flood plains to ease the ever-increasing need for homes around the country. A fallen blackberry or the root of a dogged nettle from next door would puncture their way through the weed suppressant matting to colo-nise the gap between the house and garage. Like all persistent plants they would patiently wait until the occupant either left or gave up the need to prune and spray. Also lying in wait would be the levelled willow under the gravel. Its harshly coppiced trunk would reshoot from the base amongst the safety of the nettle and bramble to tower over them as in years past.

Just maybe the new occupants would embrace their free tree amongst the bramble, allow it to grow, and harvest the blackberries in late summer. If they were partial to nettle tea then they were on to a winner. Highly unlikely, methinks, but stranger things have happened in the fickle world of humankind. Perhaps another war would make them appreciate nature's harvest?

Wake-up call

For many years I had relied on people finding me work, so when the work dried up I was left in the lurch without any particular direction. A rumour or promise of a start up north or down south were just false hopes, and to be honest I really got fed up with all the travelling, early starts and late returns without any really fruitful production in my life. Certain things also contribute to your life's path through unsuspecting jolts of loss and hardship, so it's time to think, Mark, what's it all about? Knuckle down and concentrate on what really matters. Gardens have always been my release, my refuge, my personal Elysium; we all come and go but the plants carry on regardless. They, like Quercus and co, are the immortals. Once our seed is spent or blocked we cease to exist – my seed dies with me but hey, I have plenty of nieces and nephews courtesy of my family's lively activity to carry things on ... Legacies and generations of humans will continue to grow and weaken, and who wants to live forever anyway? How boring is that!

Modern people are just distant echoes of the ancient tribes who were once there. Many lived and died on that mound of rock forced up by centuries of continental shifts. If I was to carry on doing what I loved, I had to embrace some form of ethical code for how I plant, how I work the ground, and not expecting too much from life – *The Woodcutter's Story* taught me that. Friendship and loyalty bring a better future for me than fame and fortune. Getting all the rubbish out of my life midway has meant that I can enjoy the other half with no misconceptions or fanciful dreams. Surely being known locally as a great gardener is better than being known globally as a plastic TV gardener. And yes, I should have charged more for my time when I heard of blokes earning up to £1,000 a week on just grass cutting, a bloody boring job with a braindead attitude. And yes, I did become a designer and charged for my drawings, as that in itself is a niche market, but who wants to sit in front of a drawing board all day? Just as boring as cutting grass for a living.

Family values

The art of communication is, well, a dying art unless you count the phonetic codes of text-speak on a mobile phone, which brings me back to the hillside and to a human family who wanted to spend some time together after a large Sunday dinner. Their choice of location was the hillside, but they decided to cut down the time of endurance together by driving half the way. Imagine the scene: a family or four in a pristine motor wishing to have some quality time together on the orders of a TV chat show celebrity, the car all waxed and polished with a smelly tree hanging from the mirror. Two kids in the back, both on their mobile phones: a daughter with an attitude and a son going through his early Kevin years, headphones and hoodies blocking out their parents' eyes and words of wisdom. Two loving parents in the front arguing over the choice of radio station; well at least they were talking to each other, given that the dad had been out all night on the lash. The mother trying to involve the kids in a conversation about music and fashion, only to be frowned upon. Mum all the same was confident she could get them to smile and interact as a family once again. Dad was just keen to do as she pleased and get home to watch the footie. Suddenly Mum spoke out and said that they were going for a walk up the hill today and you will bloody well enjoy yourselves. Dad grunted, the kids just sighed, such were the tribal noises coming from their mouths.

They parked up in a muddy car park on a windy day. Mum was the only one prepared for the walk with her colourful wellies and thick coat, while the rest had their hoodies and trendy trainers on. Mobile phones and head-phones off, they all reluctantly made the climb up the steep slope. Corylus was the first to spot this small tribe of people walking very slowly up the once quarry site, and given that she had witnessed many a keen walker up the hill her attention was drawn to this rabble as they were more fun to watch. They all in turn avoided a low branch followed by a bramble stem, before losing their footing on the slippery rock. Together though they caught each other and avoided going for a burton on the floor – ah, team-work and caring was present after all amongst this tribe of lost souls. The sticky patch negotiated, they walked on up the green pasture of the hillside where the wind was more forceful, and suddenly it caught all their hoods to reveal their greasy and stuck up Sunday morning hair. They all looked at each other, initially with a small smile, followed by a chuckle or laugh. Such happiness reminded them all of their childhood upbringing before ignorance and boredom took the place of fun and togetherness. Mum's hair was the biggest butt of all their jokes as it spiralled out of control in a wild banshee way. Dad's was short and partially receding, which only made the kids smile more as his slap head shiny forehead glistened in the sun.

As for the kids, well thank heavens it's Sunday and bath day, as a week of gel and hairspray had made them look like a couple of troll dolls without the purple hair colouring. A bond began to appear that had been unseen for many years. Corylus smiled as their unity was starting to get stronger as they all trudged up the windy slope, hands held with a combined support for each other to make the climb more bearable. Where once had been the Roman temple, a small entrance appeared into the wood. Intrigued, they all entered, and as the wind dropped their hoods stayed down. This moment of time opened their ears to the woodland sounds of birds and rustling leaves. Which way now, they asked each other. Mum being the head of the ramble naturally chose the path to the south towards the sun. Fraxinus caught his first sight of the family as they all shared a joke about the state of their muddy trainers and choice of clothing; the daughter seemed to be bonding with her mum again, with the dad making a small gesture to his son. Together they all looked up to the trees as the morning sun glistened through the canopy. Fraxinus watched as they stumbled down the rocky path holding on to each other, with Dad taking most of the weight of them all in a rugby scrum of hoodies and jumpers. Fraxinus laughed to himself as they were all propelled forward suddenly due to one of his slippery roots showing no favour to a slippery trainer. As they reached the bottom of the ridge their pace was slowed by the muddy track that led to the eastern gate-house of the hill fort, and a display board would provide the family with all the information they needed about the hillside's past.

Wow, they all thought, we didn't know about the hill fort just outside our back yard, and along with the nature reserve and the tales of past tribes, suddenly the hill got more interesting than any website read at home. Quercus caught sight of them all and welcomed them to their home, and as he was the only tree standing within the wood's junction point it seemed natural for the family to head towards him. The tribe at this point had their heads full of Romans and warriors, all wrapped up in a childlike mental-ity as they became the braves of the hill with sticks and twigs mimicking swords and knives. The trees had witnessed both play fighting and real fighting over the centuries, but this mock re-enactment only made them smile with memories of times long gone. As they all reached Quercus the footpath split four ways, and with the warriors positioned on one path each and standing facing Quercus, they all looked at each other and telepathi-cally all thought the same thing. They joined hands around Quercus in a joint tree hug. Perhaps mum and dad were two of the original tree hugging teenagers some years back? Quercus came over all emotional and shook some of his leaves over them in a confetti of thanks, and they all looked up and laughed. What a truly joyous bonding moment, helped along by all the trees of the hillside. From that day forward the family shared many special moments together, not only on the hillside but at home and in the car. By fate or by chance it happened, but the trees of our beloved hillside know so much more than we are led to believe.

As the family made their way down the hillside, they jointly agreed where their future paths might lead, the daughter becoming a doctor with the son being an architect, while mum and dad … well, they were just Mum and Dad – surely the best outcome for all the family.

My arrival back up the hillside

I'm a great believer in fate to help guide my uncertain path throughout my life, along with the odd jolt to keep me on the straight and narrow. We can't predict our future but we can certainly have options and choices to mull over, and an impulsive decision can either be a brilliant thing or a bad thing. Rest assured I take the rough with the smooth … Analogy over, I can announce my eventual return to the hillside.

From a friend to a friend who knew someone from down the pub: 'Oh he's very good, knows his stuff, what's his name? Drives that ancient van and has won some awards for his design work. Anyway here's his number I got from someone, written down on the back of a fag packet. He's a proper old-school gardener.'

Right, after all that, when eventually asked if I would consider having a look around this garden on the edge of a hillside I was immediately intrigued as to where exactly it was. Their directions only confirmed my suspicions of its rough location. So when I drove up the steep lane towards the house, suddenly a lifetime of memories flooded back: the time when I got caught on the barbed wire fence looking for Christmas trees, the times when I used to walk there with Pupsy, oh and that chance fall to the ground all those decades ago. So I had a lot on my mind as I drove up the lane. I went slowly, believe you me!

The house revealed itself gently amongst the early spring shoots, and I was accompanied by a tunnel of hazel as I drove ever closer to my childhood play area. I was greeted warmly by the owner of the house.

Quercus, Fraxinus and Corylus also welcomed me with open leaf and branch, while the meadow plants waited patiently in the hedgerows to be reintroduced back home. All manner of insects and birds suddenly had a warm feeling of recognition, and wondered if things might be about to get better. As I walked up the footpath suddenly the stars and planets aligned to make this day a special day – that few seconds on a universal scale was a lifetime in the planet's history.

The final words from Quercus for this day were, 'I have a great feeling about today and for the days that lie ahead. Our shambolic tapestry has begun to be resewn back to its original roots in time.'

So began another chapter in the hillside's history, yet to be written down. But that would be another book …

* * * * * * *

Afterword

So fast forward to the present day. I walk the hillside slowly, breathing in the moment and trying to recall my very distant memories. I avoid any deep muddy puddles and step cautiously onto solid rock – age and wisdom had taught me not to get my boots dirty and to avoid any slip-ups. Oh how youth is so uncomplicated. By breathing in my surroundings I'm able not only to live in the moment but also to absorb my surroundings. A freeze frame moment peering into the stem of a nettle shows me the multitude of insects living and eating in what appears to be a peaceful existence.

I look at places that were familiar to me in my childhood and take a deep breath of appreciation. From afar the old village seems calm and peaceful, but like the insects on the nettle, appearances can be deceptive. I spot the churches and the schools and feel the warmth and sadness they share amongst the community. The roar of the motorway is present along with the gentle breeze on my face. This is normality in a world full of fast lives. At that moment I realise that wellbeing and mindfulness had perhaps always been present in my life if I'd cared to find them. Like my beloved hillside they are embedded in my soul.

The hillside is lush and green and alive with birds and wildlife. Many people walk the woods now; their footprints in the bare earth are a testament to that, along with the dogs, foxes and deer. This only highlights the fact that we all share the same path in life and tread the odd muddy puddle from time to time.

Sadly some trees have been lost. Quercus, I miss you, and your wisdom and empathy for others. Such a strong, robust tree, you epitomised everything that is good about nature. Fraxinus and Corylus were never quite the same after his passing, but their grief helped the smaller saplings and trees understand that everything is not eternal. Stars explode and people die. It's a fact of life. And anyway, who wants to live forever? Certainly not me. Seeds are sown and babies are born. Surely that in itself is eternal, and as Quercus's saplings were all around him when he fell, his presence and aura was with them for weeks afterwards. Just enough time for all the trees on the hillside to adjust, grieve and move on. Inevitably there will be another king of the wood. The passage of time will determine this through natural selection. I shed a tear!

Quercus, your seed still grows on in the wood. Fraxinus and Corylus are worn and weary but hold the memories of centuries past within their roots.

As I stand here a lot older and greyer, I'm surrounded by my friends of the hillside. From gardener to horticulturist and then designer, I remain the same person but have gained a wealth of knowledge and respect for my fellow cousins, both human and plant.

Let's try not to upset the apple cart but let nature do its own thing, because after all, we all end up the same.

The End

BV - #0028 - 060821 - C0 - 228/152/10 - PB - 9781913675141